University of Oxford

Questions and Exercises for Classical Scholarships, Second Division

University of Oxford

Questions and Exercises for Classical Scholarships, Second Division

ISBN/EAN: 9783337178802

Printed in Europe, USA, Canada, Australia, Japan

Cover: Foto ©Paul-Georg Meister /pixelio.de

More available books at **www.hansebooks.com**

QUESTIONS AND EXERCISES

FOR

CLASSICAL SCHOLARSHIPS

SECOND DIVISION

(1) *HISTORICAL AND GENERAL QUESTIONS*
(2) *SUBJECTS FOR ENGLISH ESSAYS*

FOR THE USE OF SCHOOLS AND PRIVATE STUDENTS

Oxford
JAMES THORNTON, HIGH STREET
1879

PREFACE.

THE Papers and Essays in the present volume have, with very few exceptions, been set in Examinations for Scholarships at Oxford during the last decade, 1869–1879. A student will readily gather from them a correct idea of the sort of information which is required from him in these examinations. As this book, like its immediate predecessor, is adapted for the use of schools as well as private students, the compiler ventures to suggest a few hints, gathered from much experience, as to the way in which it may be used with most advantage. The private student, whether reading by himself or with a tutor, should make a practice of entering terse and accurate answers in a note-book kept for this purpose. It cannot be too urgently impressed upon him that such a note-book, unless he be gifted with a memory like Macaulay's, will be practically of no service, will even be of dis-service to him, unless he peruse and re-peruse it weekly, or even oftener—'decies repetita manebunt.' He should also make a practice of finding out on the map every name as it arises, and of carefully noting every important date. For geography and chronology are the wings of history. Without them the student cannot fly, nor can he walk even, or crawl, except in 'darkness visible,' and in a maze 'without a plan.'

In schools where written answers are sent up weekly, the use of this book as a time-saver for tutors and pupils will be obvious. It may also be profitably used in oral teaching. A competent teacher of history and geography may, with the aid of a wall map or of an atlas in the hands of each of his pupils, do much, with one weekly lesson only, to make his class respectably proficient in subjects where ignorance is as deplorable as it is common. Such a teacher cannot go over the same ground much too often; and his attention may, in the first instance, be directed to those questions which, in one form or another, 'regurgitate' so frequently in the following papers.

With respect to the Essays, the student will do well to supply references to the other subjects, similar to those which are appended here to the first six. It is for this purpose that so much space has been left in this part of the volume; and also because the compiler has found, from experience, that a list of Essay subjects printed closely together is by no means so useful as it might theoretically appear to be. An excellent custom prevails in many schools of arguing the pros and cons of various questions in the School Debating Society. The compiler would strenuously urge youthful debaters to select their subjects for debate from the questions and essays in this book, and above all to 'fight their battles o'er again,' on the same subject, half after half, or term after term. They will most assuredly find their account in doing so.

OXFORD, *May* 1879.

CONTENTS.

HISTORICAL AND GENERAL QUESTIONS.

                                                                             PAGE
I.—CXXI. PAPERS   1

SUBJECTS FOR ENGLISH ESSAYS.

I.—LX. SUBJECTS   103

QUESTIONS AND EXERCISES

FOR

CLASSICAL SCHOLARSHIPS.

SECOND DIVISION.

HISTORICAL AND GENERAL QUESTIONS.

I.

1. Compare the Greek and English languages as vehicles of thought.

2. Compare Homer and Virgil in respect of their employment of (1) metaphors, (2) epithets.

3. Compare the political and social state of North and South Greece in ancient times.

4. What effect had the Persian wars on the Hellenic world?

5. Explain the formation and character of the Roman Senate. In what sense can it be said to have been a representative assembly?

6. 'Quis tulerit Gracchos de seditione querentes?' Is the implied view of the Gracchi a fair one?

7. Describe the mode in which the House of Commons has gradually extended its power.

8. How far did the Saxon and Norman elements of our language become fused into one race?

9. Give a short life of the Sultan Saladin.

II.

1. Paraphrase and comment on the following passage:

In arts mechanical the first deviser comes shortest, and time addeth and perfecteth; but in science the first author goeth farthest, and time leeseth and corrupteth. Whereof the reason is no other, but that in the former many wits and industries have contributed in one; and in the latter many wits and industries have been spent about the wit of some one, whom many times they have rather depraved than illustrated. For as water will not ascend higher than the level of the first spring-head from whence it decendeth, so knowledge derived from Aristotle, and exempted from liberty of examination, will not rise again higher than the level of Aristotle. And therefore, although the position be good, *Oportet discentem credere*, yet it must be coupled with this, *Oportet edoctum judicare*; for disciples do owe unto masters only a temporary belief and a suspension of their own judgment until they be fully instructed, and not an absolute resignation or perpetual captivity: and therefore to concede this point, I will say no more, but, so let great authors have their due, as time which is the author of authors be not deprived of his due, which is further and further to discover truth.

2. Explain and comment on the following words and phrases: 'society'—'optimism'—'sense'—'cynicism'—'the golden mean'—'moral courage.'

3. Criticise briefly any *two* of the following authors: Pascal, Wordsworth, Macaulay, Thackeray, Schiller.

4. Can any ancient author be said to have had a strong sense of the beauty of nature, or is the feeling wholly modern?

5. The chief reasons for and against anonymous writing.

6. Compare the English, Scotch, and Irish character.

III.

1. How do Herodotus and Thucydides respectively treat the myths and early history of Greece? What data have we for determining how far Herodotus was in advance of his predecessors in respect of critical discernment?

2. Give a brief history of Roman tragedy, and estimate the influence, direct and indirect, of the Grecian drama upon the literature of Rome.

3. Compare the powers of the executive at Athens and Sparta in the fifth century A.C.

4. The history and justification of the Revolution of the Four Hundred at Athens (A.C. 411), and the characters of the chief actors therein.

5. Note the principal events in the history of the following places: Miletus, Cyrene, Tarentum, Capua.

6. Indicate the greatest crises in the military history of Rome in the period A.C. 510–367.

7. Describe carefully the system of provincial administration employed by Rome in the sixth and seventh centuries of the city. What securities were there against the abuse of power on the part of the local governors?

8. Draw a contrast between any two of the great English poets.

IV.

1. Who were Wycliff, General George Monk, Richelieu, Velasquez, Galileo?

2. Mention any important events you may remember in the reigns of the first and last kings of the line of Stuart.

3. Estimate the advantages and disadvantages of England's insular position.

4. The effect of slavery on the dominant class.

5. 'Est finitimus oratori poeta.' Show clearly how poetry and oratory agree and differ.

6. The characteristics and the use of good novels.

7. Criticise:

   (a) 'I bridle in my struggling muse with pain,
   That longs to launch into a bolder strain.'
   Addison.

   (b) 'The report is that he should have said in confidence, that he would never bear arms against him.'—*Hume.*

   (c) 'An I might live to see thee married, I have my wish.'

8. Explain carefully 'an epigram.' What is its use? Explain the following in the light of your definition:

   (a) 'He surpassed himself.'
   (b) 'The irresistible logic of facts.'
   (c) 'Nothing is so fallacious as facts, except figures.'—*Canning.*
   (d) 'The legendary age was a past that was never present.'—*Grote.*
   (e) 'Sensation is sensation.'—*Johnson.*

9. Give an outline of the history of Sicily.

V.

1. Illustrate the influence of physical conditions on the history of a nation.

2. Athens, Rome, Venice, Florence, the United States, have all been called republics. What characteristics have they in common, and what are the chief differences in their republicanism?

3. Describe the political position of Pericles, Caius Gracchus, and Julius Cæsar.

4. The variations in the military tactics of the nations of antiquity.

5. Sketch briefly the struggle between Kings and Parliaments from the reign of Henry III. to the beginning of that of Charles I.

6. Compare England and France at the end of the fifteenth century.

7. What were the chief political changes made by the English Revolution of 1688?

8. What main changes have there been in the causes of European wars in the last four centuries?

9. Sketch and estimate the political career of the two Pitts.

VI.

1. In what sense are the following sayings true?—
  (*a*) Extremes meet.
  (*b*) Summum jus summa injuria.
  (*c*) The paradox of one age is the truism of the next.

2. What is meant by Free Trade and Protection? State the arguments used on either side.

3. The constitutional sovereign 'reigns but does not govern.' What does this mean, and what is the kind of influence which belongs to the constitutional monarch?

4. Explain accurately the following: casuistry—sceptic—natural selection—deduction—induction.

5. Compare Æschylus and Euripides, Horace and Catullus, Keats and Shelley.

6. A short account of the life and works of any of the following: Dante, Pascal, Goethe, Voltaire, Defoe, Wordsworth.

VII.

1. What is the meaning of the following sayings, and in what sense are they true?—

   (a) πλέον ἥμισυ παντός.
   (b) Exceptio probat regulam.
   (c) Truth is stranger than fiction.

2. Distinguish accurately: wisdom—prudence—common sense: metaphor—simile—illustration: legal—equitable — constitutional: monarchy—royalty — sovereignty: republic—democracy—commonwealth.

3. In what characteristic does the literature of Ancient Greece most resemble or differ from that of England?

4. Is Prose or Poetry the earliest form of literature? Give reasons for your answer.

5. Show how Philology contributes to historical discovery.

6. A short account of the life and works of any of the following:—St. Bernard, Machiavelli, Spenser, Mil-

ton, Schiller, Molière. Give at the same time an outline of the period in which your author lived.

7. The causes and consequences of the Seven Years' War.

VIII.

1. Define the following words: Self-evident, crisis, barbarous, cycle, illusion.

2. On what principle would you distinguish between plagiarism and legitimate imitation.

3. 'Has life so little store of real woes
That here ye come to taste fictitious grief?'

Do you consider this a valid objection to tragedy as a species of entertainment?

4. Through what means have the Popes of Rome acquired their spiritual supremacy?

5. By what races were the Roman provinces invaded in the decline of the Empire? Which of them made permanent settlements?

6. Describe the arbitrary government of the Stuart Kings of England. In what way was it more oppressive than that of the Tudors?

7. What evils in the republic did Caius and Tiberius Gracchus attempt to remedy?

8. How did Athens acquire its maritime supremacy?

9. Describe shortly the career of Epaminondas, Julian, Saladin, Sixtus V.

IX.

1. State some of the causes of the French Revolution of 1789.

2. 'Such was the policy which brought the heir of a long line of kings to a prison and a scaffold.' What policy? Contrast (with facts) his policy with that of Queen Elizabeth.

3. What was the 'Habeas Corpus' Act? When did it become law? And what was the Toleration Act?

4. Can you mention some results of the impetus given to English civilisation by the expulsion of the House of Stuart?

5. Discuss briefly one or more of the following subjects:

    (a) The comparative merits of classical and romantic poetry.
    (b) The equitable rights of a tenant over the land he occupies.
    (c) The effects of music, *or* of the drama, on national character.
    (d) The value of history as a training for the mind.
    (e) The disadvantages of public school education.
    (f) The comparative merits of Classical and Gothic architecture.

X.

1. What was the Feudal system, and what was its origin in Europe? Give the meaning of the word 'Feudal.'

2. Who were the Normans? Give a short account of their conquests in Europe.

3. Show how the different classes of English society were affected by the Conquest, and give some account of the early life and of the character of William the Conqueror.

4. Give the date of the capture of Constantinople by the Turks; mention some of the effects of that capture (1) upon the political state of Europe, (2) upon letters.

5. Was the loss of France a benefit to England, or the contrary? Give reasons for your answer.

6. Which was the most powerful of the European nations in the sixteenth century? What was the extent of its dominion, and what its policy?

7. The measures which led to the rupture with the American Colonies: what statesmen are responsible for them?

8. Give the date of Charlemagne; his character, policy, and the extent of his dominions.

9. Give the dates and characteristics of the following: Kings Henry II. and Henry VII. of England, Archbishop Cranmer, Lord Burleigh, Cardinal Richelieu, Lord Falkland, Lord Clarendon, Talleyrand, Lord Palmerston.

10. Write a short account of the Duke of Buckingham satirized in 'Absolom and Achitophel,' and give Dryden's lines upon him.

XI.

1. The rise of the Athenian ascendency in Greece.

2. The manner in which the various magistracies of republican Rome were united in the emperor.

3. Give some account of Solon, Aristides, Appius Claudius Cæcus, and the two Catos; and of the historians Herodotus, Arrian, Sallust, and Suetonius.

4. Roman Catholicism as affecting English politics since the time of Mary.

5. The rise in England of a ministry responsible to Parliament.

6. The various races of the British Islands.

7. The struggle for power between the Crown, the nobility, and the communes in France.

8. Give an account of the progress of geographical discovery in the fifteenth and sixteenth centuries.

XII.

1. Compare the Greek and Roman religions in respect of their influence on political progress.

2. Estimate the strength of the evidence for events in Greek history before 500 B.C.

3. What causes favoured the growth of political speculation in Greece?

4. Progress has been said to be 'an advance from homogeneous to heterogeneous.' Illustrate this statement from the constitutional history of Greece and Rome.

5. Is it true to say that the Empire came too late in the history of Rome.

6. What means do we possess of forming an accurate conception of the earliest state of society in Latium?

7. Trace the influence of Oriental ideas upon Roman society under the Empire.

8. Account (1) for the brilliancy, (2) for the rapid decline of Provençal culture.

9. Connect the political theories of Dante with the state of Italy in his time.

10. Discuss the reign of Henry VIII. as an epoch in the history of the English nobility.

11. Enumerate the chief epochs in what Lord Coke calls the struggle 'between sovran power and Magna Charta.'

XIII.

1. Trace briefly the history of the Attic dialect.

2. How far may dramatic poetry be said to have flourished at Rome?

3. Illustrate the confused state of the Greek case-system. What traces of the instrumental are to be found in Greek?

4. What is meant by saying that the Romans were the first stylists?

5. What are the chief facts in the history of the Greek alphabet? What connection may be historically traced between alphabetic writing and formative art?

6. Criticise recent opinions on the Homeric question.

7. Estimate precisely the knowledge of the Greek language possessed by cultivated Romans in Cicero's day.

8. What indications are there of the influence of accent upon Latin versification?

9. The literary history of the Greek anthology.

10. What information may be gained respecting ancient Greek life and character from (1) their personal names, (2) their every-day metaphors?

XIV.

1. Compare the character and political position of Charlemagne and Napoleon the Great.

2. In what ways has the modern world been most influenced by classical antiquity?

3. Give a short account, with dates, of *any two* of the following: Gonsalvo de Cordova, Richelieu, Epaminondas, St. Boniface of Germany, Tiberius Gracchus, Lord Burleigh.

4. Sketch briefly the Thirty Years' War, *or* the Peloponnesian War, *or* the contest between Pompey and Cæsar.

5. Distinguish between a serf and a slave, between the title of emperor and king, between the Roman 'colonia' and the modern 'colony.'

6. Explain the failure of the Crusades.

7. What events do you connect with the names of Rocroi, Ravenspur, Northallerton, Artemisium, Marengo, the Savoy Hospital? Give dates.

8. Why has the union between England and Scotland proved more prosperous than that between England and Ireland?

9. Compare the relation between the different classes of society in the middle of the eighteenth century in England and France.

10. Are Shakespeare's views of English history at all influenced by the ideas of the time in which he wrote? Has he contributed to spread erroneous views on the subject?

11. At what point in Athenian history can her constitution be said to have become a complete democracy?

12. Explain the skill of the Romans in making, organising, and retaining their conquests.

XV.

1. Give a paraphrase and a brief explanation of the following passage:

'We see then that it is so far from being true, that all moral good and evil, just and unjust (if these be anything), are made by mere will and arbitrary commands (as many conceive), that it is not possible that any command of God or man should oblige otherwise than by virtue of that which is naturally just. And though particular promises and commands be made by will, yet it is not will but nature that obligeth to the doing of things promised and commanded, or makes them such things as ought to be done. For mere will cannot change the moral nature of actions, nor the nature of intellectual beings. And therefore if there were no natural justice, that is, if the rational or intellectual nature in its self were indetermined and unobliged to do anything, and so destitute of all morality, it were not possible that anything should be made morally good or evil, obligatory or unlawful, or that any moral obligation should be begotten by any will or command whatsoever.'

2. Distinguish between demonstrative proof and moral certainty, rhetoric and eloquence, mechanical and chemical combination.

3. What is the highest law in astronomical science, and upon what kind of evidence is the law based?

4. Characterise and distinguish between selfishness, self-esteem, self-respect, and self-consciousness.

5. Into what periods would you divide the history of English literature?

6. Give a criticism of the works of any eminent prose writer of the seventeenth century.

7. Contrast the characteristic excellences of Greek and Gothic architecture.

XVI.

1. What has been the influence of the physical geography of Greece on its history?

2. Contrast the relations of Persia to Greece before and after the Peloponnesian War.

3. What were the legislative, executive, judicial, and social measures of Pericles' administration?

4. What were the various steps by which the Roman franchise was extended to the Italians?

5. Describe the various functions of the elective and legislative bodies of Rome.

6. State what you know of Spurius Cassius, Appius Claudius Cæcus, Tiberius and Caius Gracchus.

7. Contrast the religions of Egypt, Greece, and Italy.

8. Compare the condition of slaves and of the working classes in ancient and modern times.

9. 'The English and French wars of the Middle Ages lasted for 120 years for a prize which was twice gained and twice lost.' Comment on this statement.

10. Account for the divergence in the histories of England, Spain, and France as regards their representative assemblies.

11. What was the effect of the Crusades on Europe?

12. How far is Shakespeare trustworthy as an historical authority?

XVII.

1. What is the date of the Revival of Letters in Europe, and who were the principal leaders in it?

2. What is the design of the 'Faery Queene'? What does Milton say about Spenser and Cromwell and Shakespeare? What other writers in the Spenserian stanza can you mention?

3. What was Milton's design in the 'Allegro' and 'Penseroso'? Do you know any writer to whom he is indebted for many hints in these two poems? Quote any one of his sonnets.

4. Compare the prose style of Swift with that of Johnson.

5. Give a short sketch of the life of Addison. What other contributors to the 'Spectator' can you mention?

6. Derivation of the following: Biscuit, Lammas, galaxy, cynosure, pamphlet, tinsel, colonel, constable, sheriff, marquis.

7. What is the usual termination of adverbs in (1) English and in (2) French, and what does it mean?

8. Whence come the following? Give the context where you can:

> (*a*) Shakespeare could not have written an epic: he would have died of a plethora of thought.
>
> (*b*) Sporting the lion ramped, and in his paw
> Dandled the kid.

To whom has this last quotation been applied?

> (*c*) He nothing common did, or mean,
> Upon that memorable scene.
>
> (*d*) Nature's sternest painter, but her best.
>
> (*e*) Winter barricades the realms of frost.

(*f*) Forbade to wade through slaughter to a throne.

(*g*) The holy texts of pike and gun.

9. The history of the reign of Augustus, illustrated from the Latin poets.

XVIII.

1. Should moral duties be enforced by law?

2. Estimate the disadvantages of party government.

3. Ostracism considered as a political institution.

4. 'The battle of Marathon, even as an event in English history, is more important than the battle of Hastings.' Explain and criticise this.

5. What have been the influences, direct or indirect, of Scott's novels?

6. Discuss the utility of classical verse composition.

7. Explain the bearing and historical connection (if any) of—

(*a*) πλέον ἥμισυ παντός.
(*b*) Rex nunquam moritur.
(*c*) Rex non potest peccare.
(*d*) Summum jus summa injuria.
(*e*) Verbosity is cured by a wide vocabulary.
(*f*) Nature, like liberty, is best restrained
    By the same laws which first herself ordained.

XIX.

1. At what date do you fix the beginning of modern history, and why?

2. Compare the judicial systems of Athens and Rome.

3. Sketch the origin of the English system of parliamentary representation.

4. Define a republic; and distinguish its meaning in application to Switzerland, the United Provinces, Poland, Athens, Rome, Venice.

5. Give a biography of *any two* of the following: Conon, Philopœmen, Otho, Wiclif, Dante, Wallenstein, Lord Clive, Lafayette.

6. Give instances of departure from the Mosaic law by the Jews of our Lord's time.

7. The character of St. Paul as shown in (1) the Acts, (2) his Epistles.

8. Point out and comment on any differences between the grammar of the New Testament and of classical Greek.

9. To what extent has the character of the Christian Church been permanently determined by the decrees of the first four general councils?

10. What is the value of the argument from undesigned coincidences? Give examples from the Old Testament.

XX.

1. How was the place of the modern press supplied (1) in ancient Athens, (2) in ancient Rome?

2. How far was the Roman emperor a reproduction of the Roman king?

3. The political theory of Virgil and of Horace.

4. The attempts made before Cæsar's to place the government of the Roman State in a single hand.

5. The influence of Alexander the Great on Asia.

6. Discuss the political character of Augustus. What appearance did it present to an ordinary Roman contemporary?

7. Trace briefly the rise and fall of the chief towns of Magna Græcia.

8. Origin and development of the House of Commons.

9. To what arguments could a Cavalier and Roundhead severally appeal in support of the cause he espoused?

10. Write a character of Cicero, *or* of Luther.

11. At what periods has the safety of Europe been endangered by Asiatic invasions?

XXI.

1. What is meant by the phrase, 'the immobility of the East'?

2. What is wanted in a Christian missionary to India?

3. The secular influence of the Western Church in the Dark Ages. Is the 'Dark Ages' a proper expression? If not, why not?

4. Why was an Italian republic in the Dark Ages less like the Roman than like a Greek republic?

5. Compare the English with the French Parliaments; and explain the saying, 'England is the mother of Parliaments.'

6. Compare Cardinal Richelieu with Oliver Cromwell.

7. The harm done by railways, steam-boats, and the electric telegraph.

8. Why have we ceased to pass sumptuary laws?

9. Can the citizens of the United States, or the greater part of them, be said to be Anglo-Saxons? If not, why not?

10. Write a proposal in the style of Lord Bacon for dealing with Ireland.

11. What do you know of Wiklif, Frederick Barbarossa, Bethlem Gabor, Washington, Colbert, Savonarola, Belisarius?

12. When and wherefore famous are Clarendon, Leipzig, Bunker's Hill, Alcala, Nuremberg, Belgrade, Chinon?

XXII.

1. Give an account of the position and influence of the Prophets in Hebrew history.

2. Compare the Spartan and Athenian constitutions.

3. At what period in the history of Rome were her political institutions most successful, and the national character at its best?

4. What evidence does the New Testament furnish as to the position of the Jews in the Roman Empire?

5. State the main provisions of Magna Charta, and point out its relations to English Constitutional History before and after it.

6. Give an account of the defeat of the Spanish Armada.

7. The character and historical importance of Louis

XI., Richelieu, William III. of England, and Frederic II. of Prussia.

8. Compare Pitt with Fox, Nelson with Wellington.

XXIII.

1. Into what main divisions are languages separated by Philology, and on what grounds?

2. The history of the Latin hexameter.

3. Compare the structure of the sentence in Greek, Latin, and English prose.

4. Give a short analysis of, and criticism on, any English poem.

5. Compare the English poetry of the eighteenth and nineteenth centuries.

6. Distinguish definition and description—simile and metaphor—aristocracy, oligarchy, nobility—right and wrong, rights and wrongs—to predicate and to predict—and explain the expressions 'begging the question'—'the exception proves the rule.'

7. Describe accurately the barometer, *or* a locomotive steam-engine.

8. Describe the government of the United States.

9. Trace the changes in the constitution of the Roman Republic, in the interval between the expulsion of the kings, and the taking of the city by the Gauls.

XXIV.

1. Trace the influence of the Phœnicians in the ancient world.

2. πολεμικοί τε καὶ εὔβουλοι διὰ τὸ εὔκοσμον γιγνόμεθα. Examine this in reference to Spartan character and policy.

3. The origin and progress of agrarian movements at Rome.

4. 'Græcia capta ferum victorem cepit, et artes
   Intulit agresti Latio.'
Illustrate this.

5. Describe the policy of Augustus, and illustrate it from Horace and Virgil.

6. What was the influence of Charlemagne in the creation of modern Europe?

7. Examine historically the use of the words 'imperator,' 'emperor,' 'empire.'

8. Sketch the gradual amalgamation of England and Scotland, and account for it.

9. Account for the following names:—Alexandria—Naples—Provence—Cologne—Venice—Britain—Essex—Chester—Whitby.

XXV.

1. What changes in the Athenian constitution are connected with the names of Solon, Cleisthenes, and Pericles respectively?

2. What were the causes of the Peloponnesian War?

3. What were the chief causes which led to the establishment of the Empire at Rome?

4. Distinguish between a federal government and confederacy, republic and democracy, hegemony and empire, with examples.

5. What do you know about Spurius Cassius, Brasidas, Philopœmen, Civilis, Hildebrand, Simon de Mont-

ford, Savonarola, Henri Quatre, Erasmus, Lamoral Egmont?

6. What principles were at stake in the resistance of the Parliament to Charles I.?

XXVI.

1. Distinguish between epic and lyric poetry. In what kinds of poetical composition does the English nation excel?

2. What languages of Modern Europe are derived from Latin? Trace the processes by which they assumed their present form.

3. How has the origin of the case-system of the Greek and Latin languages been explained?

4. Is perfect translation possible? and, if so, what rules would you give for attaining it?

5. To what kinds of literature is modern civilisation (1) favourable, (2) unfavourable?

6. Compare the early Roman with the early Greek mythology.

7. Analyse Shakespeare's conception of the following characters, illustrating by quotations:—Hamlet, Iago, Prospero, Lady Macbeth, Queen Constance, Wolsey.

8. Explain the following terms: 'Missi dominici,' 'balance of power,' 'dialectical regeneration,' 'natural selection,' 'correlation of forces,' 'spectrum analysis.'

9. State briefly what is known of the interval history, and religion, of the Persian nation.

XXVII.

1. What are the advantages and disadvantages of small States as members of the European Commonwealth?

2. Describe the Athenian democracy, as understood and developed by Cimon and Pericles.

3. Mention the chief elements of the success of Julius Cæsar.

4. Trace the influence of Roman municipal institutions on mediæval history.

5. What were the predisposing causes of the Crusades?

6. Compare the chief characteristics of the popular uprisings in England and France in the fourteenth and sixteenth centuries.

7. State the causes which hindered mediæval Italy from becoming a united kingdom.

8. Contrast the social condition of England, Australia, and Turkey.

9. Give an account of the different methods pursued by the English in the government of Ireland.

10. Compare the characters of Sir Thomas More, Erasmus, Melanchthon, the Chancellor L'Hôpital.

11. What were the most notable effects of the discovery of America on Europe, during the sixteenth century?

12. On what principles, and by what means, has Austria at different times endeavoured to take the lead in Europe?

XXVIII.

1. 'The dominion of speech is erected upon the downfall of interjections.' Explain and comment upon this.

2. 'Churl is derived from the Anglo-Saxon ceorl.' 'Minster is derived from μοναστήριον.' 'Telegraph is derived from τῆλε γράφω.' Is the word 'derived' equally applicable in all these cases? Illustrate the kinds of derivation here exemplified.

3. In respect of its origin, 'to' (in English) is not the sign of the infinitive mood. What then is it?

4. Write brief notices of the life and writings of John Gower, Roger Ascham, Sir John Davies, John Ford, Andrew Marvell, Edward Young.

5. Give the etymology and trace any variations in the meaning of the following words: instance, maxim, humour, influence, villain, gossip, kindly, circumstance.

6. To what originals was Shakespeare indebted for the subjects of his dramas? Is there any play of his the plot of which appears to be entirely his own?

7. Give an analysis of one work of each of the following writers: Lessing, Goethe, Schiller.

8. Compare the literary genius of Goethe and Schiller.

9. En quoi consiste la supériorité des historiens Français du 19me siècle sur leurs prédécesseurs?

XXIX.

1. State what you know of Theodoric, Attila, Rienzi, Hildebrand, Savonarola, Erasmus, Louis XI., Archbishop Parker, *or* Laud, *or* Tillotson, Sir John Elliott, Sir T.

Fairfax, Richelieu, Tamerlane, Zenghis Khan, Swift, Sir R. Walpole, Dr. Johnson, Jeremy Bentham.

2. The influence of the Persian War on the history and literature of Greece.

3. The geographical boundaries of Hellas.

4. The causes, nature, and results of the struggle between

  (*a*) The patricians and plebeians.
  (*b*) The Gracchi and the Senate.
  (*c*) Cæsar and the party headed by Pompey.

5. What were the chief differences between the Romans and the Greeks; and what were the points contrasting with modern peoples which they had in common?

6. Give some account of any of the following:—

  (*a*) The Holy Roman Empire between 950–1280.
  (*b*) The downfall of the empire of Spain.
  (*c*) The failure of the schemes of Louis XIV.
  (*d*) The parts played by the various European powers between 1789–1815.
  (*e*) Consequences of the French Revolution in France itself and Europe generally.

XXX.

1. What are the advantages and disadvantages to the world at large of small states in the European system?

2. Trace, and account for, the rise and decline of religious persecution in England.

3. Compare ancient Egypt and the Valley of the Ganges, both geographically, and with regard to the

character, pursuits, and social institutions of the inhabitants.

4. Contrast the Reformation in England, Scotland, and Germany.

5. Explain the following terms :—βασιλεὺς, τύραννος, imperator, Bretwalda, Holy Roman Emperor, Prester John, the Great Mogul, the Sublime Porte.

6. What were the services to civilisation of Alexander the Great, Charlemagne, and St. Lewis?

7. Give an account of the suppression of the Templars, and the rise of the Jesuits.

8. Exemplify the tendency of financial embarrassment to produce political revolution.

9. What properly constitutes a great man? Illustrate your view historically.

10. What is to be said as to the objection, that certainty in history is unattainable?

XXXI.

1. What relations generally existed between a Greek colony and its parent state?

2. Compare the systems of government pursued by the three first Cæsars.

3. Give short biographies of any two of the following :—Brasidas, Iphicrates, Polybius, C. Gracchus, Stephen Langton, Zwingle, Sir William Temple, Eugene of Savoy, Carnot.

4. Describe the foreign policy of England in the reign of Charles II.

5. Compare the position of the administration in England in the reigns of Anne—George II.—Victoria.

6. Describe the principal steps in the growth of the Prussian monarchy.

7. What were the most marked characteristics of the Athenian people? What people of modern times has most resembled it?

8. What treaties of union have there been between England, Ireland, and Scotland?

XXXII.

1. Explain: individuality — sublime — reaction — romance — communism.

2. What reasons would you give for the modern love of natural scenery? Contrast the ancient and modern feeling on this point.

3. What is the effect on a nation of the prevalence among all classes of a desire for social advancement?

4. Distinguish between truthfulness, consistency, and straightforwardness: illustrate their effects on individual character.

5. Compare Sir Walter Scott's novels with those of the present day.

6. What amount of truth is there in the following sayings?

      (*a*) Ars est celare artem.
      (*b*) Poeta nascitur, non fit.
      (*c*) No man is a hero to his valet.
      (*d*) All's well that ends well.
      (*e*) There is nothing new under the sun.

XXXIII.

1. Give a short sketch of the events between the battle of Platæa and the beginning of the Peloponnesian War. *Or*, trace the steps by which the supremacy of Macedon was established in Greece.

2. What was the process of making a law at Athens in the time of Pericles? Give the technical terms.

3. What were the chief crises in the military history of Rome down to the year 130 B.C.? Write a short account of the Second Samnite, or of the Second Punic War.

4. Give an account of the chief Roman magistracies in the time of Cicero.

5. Describe a Roman triumph. Quote passages in illustration from any Latin authors.

6. What was the origin of the English system of government by party; and what are its most conspicuous defects?

7. Give a list of the possessions of the English Crown, and state under what circumstances they were severally acquired.

8. Sketch the life, character, and policy of not more than three of the following: Miltiades, Nicias, Sulla, Tiberius, Wolsey, Pym, Halifax, Mirabeau.

9. Explain fully not more than three of the following terms: Ostracism, The Theoric Fund, Lex Majestatis, Ordo Equitum, Constituent Assembly, Declaration of Independence, East India Company, Petition of Right, Golden Bull, Act of Settlement.

10. The causes of the First French Revolution.

XXXIV.

1. Distinguish, with instances, between direct and indirect taxation.

2. The effects of primogeniture.

3. The language of a people is the unconscious record of its history. Explain and illustrate this.

4. The disadvantages of trial by jury.

5. The principal dangers of democracy.

6. Can one nation justifiably hold another in subjection?

7. Explain, and, where necessary, criticise: casuistry—a crucial test—special pleading—a legal fiction—a maxim.

> (*a*) 'The right divine to govern wrong.'
>
> (*b*) 'Potior est lectio difficilior.'
>
> (*c*) 'Can sins of moment earn the rod
>   Of everlasting fires?
>
> (*d*) Can that offend great Nature's God
>   Which Nature's self inspires?'

8. Give a short history of Corinth, enumerating its colonies.

XXXV.

1. What were the causes of the Peloponnesian War?

2. What persons attained absolute power at Rome before the time of Julius Cæsar?

3. The history of the Jewish war of Vespasian and Titus.

4. How was the English dominion increased or diminished in the reigns of Henry II., Edward I., Henry VI., Mary I., Anne, George II.

5. Some account of the Battle of Bosworth Field, the Seven Years' War, the Septennial Act, the Cabal, the Bill of Rights, the Peace of Westphalia.

6. What is meant by the 'Renaissance'? Give a sketch of the great events which distinguished that epoch.

7. The causes of the long existence of the Byzantine Empire.

8. Who were Richelieu, Strafford, Simon de Montfort, Ximenes, Earl of Chatham, Duke of Alva, Necker, Cavour?

9. A brief outline of European colonisation—

(*a*) in North America,
(*b*) in India;

and account briefly for the ultimate predominance of the Anglo-Saxon race in both countries.

10. The relations of Britain with the Roman empire.

XXXVI.

1. Compare any play of a Greek tragic poet with a play of Shakespeare.

2. How far is any Latin literature truly national?

3. What is meant by the distinction between the 'natural' and the 'artificial' epic. Illustrate from Homer, Virgil, and Milton.

4. State any facts which indicate the common origin of the myths of many of the nations of Europe and Asia.

5. Language as a record of past states of society.

6. Discuss not more than two of the following subjects:—

    (*a*) The Spectrum Analysis.
    (*b*) The Darwinian Theory.
    (*c*) The Zymotic Theory.
    (*d*) Stages in the History of Chemical Research.
    (*e*) The various theories as to the Course of Geological Change.

7. What is meant by the comparison of the life of a race or a nation to the life of the individual?

8. Exhibit the connection or contrast between any two periods of English literature with which you are acquainted.

9. The nature of the changes at work in the formation of the French or any other Romance language from Latin.

XXXVII.

1. Compare the Jewish patriarchal history with the knowledge derived from other sources of the early history of society.

2. Describe the main features of the geography of Palestine or of Italy.

3. Is the charge against the Athenian people of ingratitude to their most distinguished men borne out by facts?

4. What were the main causes of political struggles in the first two centuries of the Roman republic?

5. The attitude of our Lord and the writers in the New Testament towards the political and social arrangements of the time.

6. What were the causes of the ecclesiastical supremacy of Rome?

7. What were the questions at issue in the Wars of the Roses, or in the Revolution of 1688?

8. Trace the effects in history of the invention of gunpowder, or of printing, or of railways.

9. Can any uniformity of personal character be traced in the English kings of the Plantagenet, Tudor, or Stuart lines respectively?

10. Illustrate the influence of romance in our estimate of historical characters.

XXXVIII.

1. Give an account of the course of Greek colonisation.

2. The history of Pericles in connection with the Athenian constitution.

3. Give a short history of Thebes, or of Samos, or of Argos.

4. Trace the course of the struggle between the privileged and unprivileged classes in Rome.

5. The life and policy of Hannibal.

6. How far in forms and in essence did the Roman empire continue the republic?

7. A life of Frederick Barbarossa.

8. Account for the spread of Protestantism in Europe, and for its limitation.

9. How far was the English Revolution of 1688 an anticipation of the French Revolution of 1789?

XXXIX.

1. Give an outline of the controversy about the Letters of Phalaris, or of that on the authorship of the Homeric poems.

2. Give an analysis of some play of Shakespeare, or a description of the works of any modern poet with whom you are acquainted.

3. Define—law, equity; legal fiction; centralisation; social compact; political economy; commune; communism.

4. What is the meaning of the following?

> 'Extremes meet.' 'Proving too much.' 'A little knowledge is a dangerous thing.' 'Summum jus summa injuria.' 'Qui s'excuse s'accuse.'

5. Paraphrase the following passage:

'These are the studies wherein our noble and our gentle youth ought to bestow their time in a disciplinary way from twelve to one-and-twenty; unless they rely more upon their ancestors dead than upon themselves living. In which methodical course it is so supposed they must proceed by the steady pace of learning onward, as at convenient times for memories' sake to retire back into the middle ward, and sometimes into the rear of what they have been taught, until they have confirmed, and solidly united the whole body of their perfected knowledge, like the last embattelling of a Roman legion.'

6. The etymology and history of the words—abstemious, charity, fascination, humility, hypocrisy, pecuniary, province, romance, scepticism, sycophant, villain.

7. The merits or demerits of trial by jury.

XL.

1. The Darwinian theory of natural selection.
2. An account of the Constitution of the United States of America.
3. Compare the ancient and modern drama.
4. The merits and defects of centralisation.
5. The connection between the condition of society and the development of the various forms of literature.

XLI.

1. Trace shortly the progress of the Romans towards political equality from the beginning of the Republic till the war with Pyrrhus.
2. Give a short account of the rise and fall of the Carthaginian power in Sicily.
3. The principal events of the revolt of the Ionians of Asia Minor against the Persians.
4. The political regulations of Sulla.
5. Give short accounts of any of the following men : Brasidas, Xenophon, Q. Sertorius, Louis XI. of France, Wallenstein.
6. The merits and defects of the institutions of Sparta.
7. Trace the political development of Greece from the stage represented by Homer to that of the legislation of Cleisthenes.
8. The permanent effects of the Great Rebellion and the Commonwealth on English political history.

XLII.

1. Why were the Phœnicians, rather than the Egyptians, the earliest and most enterprising ocean navigators?

2. Specify the characteristics of Bœotia, and its place in Greek history.

3. At what points do the Jews appear prominently in history since the time of our Lord?

4. How far can China be properly called a highly-civilised country?

5. How far were the Wars of the Roses produced or affected in their character by the great Anglo-French war?

6. Trace the steps by which William III. secured the throne of England, and sketch his character.

7. Compare the influence on political movements of the philosophical writers of England in the seventeenth century, with that of those of France in the eighteenth century.

8. Describe the border-lands between Germany and France, and show the importance of particular positions from a military point of view.

9. Account for: (*a*) the long resistance of Jugurtha to the Romans; (*b*) Bonaparte's failure in his Russian campaign; (*c*) the overthrow of the English in Affghanistan.

10. Explain the following: the Danish Burghs; the Foul Raid; the Day of the Spurs; the Black Death; the King of Bourges; the Winter-King; a bed of justice; a joyous entrance.

XLIII.

1. 'Instances of national rejuvenescence are rare in the annals of the world.' Examine this statement and illustrate from history.

2. What have been the characteristics and influence on history of the principal nomad races?

3. 'The ruler must rule by fear.' What success has this maxim had in ancient and modern times?

4. Explain the following terms:—Patriarchal theory of government — Cæsarism — social compact — communism.

XLIV.

1. Give a paraphrase and a brief explanation of the following passage:—

'Now Pursuit and Refusal in the Will do follow, the one the Affirmation, the other the Negation of Goodness; which the Understanding apprehendeth, grounding itself upon Sense, unless some higher Reason do chance to teach the contrary. And if Reason have taught it rightly to be good, yet not so apparently, that the Mind receiveth it with utter impossibility of being otherwise; still there is place left for the Will to take or leave. Whereas, therefore, amongst so many things as are to be done, there are so few the goodness whereof Reason in such sort doth, or easily can discover, we are not to marvel at the choice of evil, even when the contrary is probably known.'

2. Compare the ancient and modern conceptions of the qualities which go to make up a great man.

3. Is a man bound to keep a promise extorted by fear?

4. 'By an obvious transposition of ideas, some persons have confounded a knowledge of useful things with useful knowledge.' Discuss the attacks which have been made on classical education.

5. Give an analysis of the plot of one of Shakespeare's plays.

6. 'If men will impartially, and not asquint, look towards the offices and function of a poet, they will easily conclude to themselves the impossibility of any man's being the good poet without first being a good man.' Examine this statement.

XLV.

1. In which of the great divisions of governments would you place the constitution of Sparta?

2. The causes which made Athens the centre of Greek culture.

3. The effect of the personal character of leading statesmen upon the issue of the Peloponnesian War.

4. The question at issue in the Social War of 90 B.C.

5. Sketch the character of any of the following:— Sulla, Pompey, Tiberius, Germanicus, Claudius.

6. Contrast Norman and English national character at the time of the death of Edward the Confessor.

7. Consider Catherine of Medicis, Elizabeth Tudor, and Mary Stuart, as illustrating the state of politics and society in their age.

8. Comment on the peculiar character and policy, throughout mediæval and modern times, of the republic of Venice.

9. Point out how we may take Cromwell, Marl-

borough, and Wellington, each as a typical British soldier of his time.

10. How far does the history of the capital city in Italy, France, England, and Russia illustrate and reflect the character and ambition of the nation?

XLVI.

1. Give, with dates, a brief history of the extension of the Roman dominion over Italy.

2. Trace briefly the growth of the Athenian hegemony.

3. The political bearings of the Athenian drama.

4. 'The United Kingdom of Great Britain and Ireland.' Explain this expression historically.

5. What share has the Papacy had in advancing or retarding civilisation?

6. Compare any two of the following authors :—Pope, Byron, Wordsworth, Tennyson.

7. What do we know of the history of Spain up to the time when it became a Roman province?

XLVII.

1. Discuss the following characters :—The Prometheus of Æschylus; the Hamlet of Shakespeare; the Arthur of Tennyson.

2. What do you understand by consistency, sublimity, style?

3. Illustrate the ideas of beauty from ancient and modern poets.

4. What reasons are there for supposing that instinct is an accumulation of habits transmitted hereditarily?

5. Give an outline of the history of British rule in India.

6. Cicero as a politician and literary man.

7. Compare French and Athenian character.

8. What was the Renaissance?

9. How is society affected by the disuse of wearing arms?

10. In what sense are colonies useful to the mother-country?

XLVIII.

1. Write short notices of the life and writings of Goldsmith, Defoe, Swift, and Steele.

2. Give the derivation of the following words, explaining fully, in the case of compounds, the meaning of each part: jeopardy, worship, wretchlessness, eyrie, coxswain, squirrel, become, crimson, forlorn, cobweb, caterer.

3. 'The French and Germans have named the vowels, but the English have nicknamed them.' Comment on this statement.

4. By what arguments would you try to prove that English belongs to the Indo-European family of languages? With what subdivision of this family does it seem most closely connected? Give reasons for your answer.

5. Explain the following passages:

    (*a*) And being fap, sir, was, as they say, cashiered; and so conclusions passed the careires.

    (*b*) Ford's a knave, and I will aggravate his style.

(c) How may likeness made in crimes,
    Mocking practise on the times,
    To draw with idle spider's strings
    Most ponderous and substantial things!

(d) There is an eyry of children, like eyases, that cry out on top of question.

(e) I fetch my life and being
    From men of royal siege; and my demerits
    May speak, unbonneted, to as proud a fortune
    As this that I have reached.

(f) This piping time of peace.

6. Show that the influence of Boileau on the tone of literary composition is as clearly manifest in England as it was in France.

7. Compare the literary genius of Shakespeare and Molière.

8. Explain how it happened that some Latin words like *adjutare, ministerium, sollicitare,* &c., have become in French *aider* and *ajouter, métier* and *ministère, soucier* and *solliciter,* &c.

9. Give what you know of the history of the Académie Française.

10. Compare the 'Iphigénie' of Racine with that of Euripides.

11. What are the qualities which, according to Hallam, 'distinguish the French tongue above all others with which we are acquainted, and render allowable a comparison between it and the Latin'?

12. Give some account of the source and history of the 'Nibelungen Lied,' and give a short sketch of its story.

13. What is the literary history of Germany from 1720 to 1760?

14. When did Klopstock, Lessing, Goethe, Jean Paul

Richter live? Notice briefly their literary work and character.

15. Give a short sketch of Schiller's life and works.

XLIX.

1. 'Property should make law for property, and persons for persons.' Comment on this.

2. The advantages and disadvantages of anonymous authorship in journalism.

3. 'C'est une erreur singulière entre toutes les erreurs humaines que d'avoir cru que dans les cités anciennes l'homme jouissait de la liberté. Il n'en avait pas même l'idée.' How far is this true?

4. Examine the position that 'the more perfect civilisation is, the less occasion has it for government.'

5. From what causes did the Greeks fail to produce any system of jurisprudence?

6. The proper function of the imagination in writing history.

7. It has been said, that 'there is no better help towards a true apprehension of the English poetry of the eighteenth century than a knowledge of the poetry of Augustan Rome.' Illustrate this.

8. The conception of Fate in Homer, Æschylus, and Shakespeare.

L.

1. Exemplify the influence of geography in the development of political institutions.

2. Contrast slavery in classical times and in modern America.

3. Why has Christianity made so little permanent impression on Orientals?

4. Illustrate historically the connection between commercial prosperity and political freedom.

5. What great passages of English history are associated with the University or Colleges of Oxford?

6. State the general causes which favoured the rise of the Italian republics in the Middle Ages.

7. What were the effects of the Great Schism upon the condition and history of the later mediæval Church?

8. Describe the character and policy of the following French kings: Philip the Fair, Louis XI., Henri Quatre.

9. Contrast the position and principles of Luther and Calvin.

10. What were the special grievances of the English people under Charles the First?

11. What improvements in the art of war were made by Gustavus Adolphus, Frederick the Second, and Bonaparte respectively?

12. How far is the possession of colonies a source of strength or weakness to the parent state?

LI.

1. Is it better for a state that the ambitious or the contented temper should prevail among its citizens?

2. How far is the critical faculty likely to be a help, and how far a hindrance, to the poet or artist?

3. What is meant by saying that a word is derived from another word, or from a root? Upon what kind of evidence does a sound derivation usually rest?

4. What effect is likely to be produced upon English literature by extending the study of modern languages, and lessening the study of Greek and Latin?

5. 'Facit natura nihil per saltum.' Explain this principle, and illustrate its application.

6. What is meant by the terms 'Classical' and 'Romantic'? Can you trace a Romantic element in Greek and Latin literature?

7. Define: property, constitution, force, economy, wealth, common sense; and point out any ambiguous uses of these words.

LII.

1. 'It is the perpetual error of the sensational school to confound the indispensable condition of a thing with the thing itself.' Examine this.

2. Give a summary of Aristotle's doctrine on reform, on the nature of law, and on the efficacy of education.

3. 'Whatever is, is right.' Comment on this statement.

4. In what sense, if any, is it true that 'the tendency of Art is polytheistic'?

5. Give some account of the Moral Philosophy of Hobbes.

6. Examine Aristotle's criticism of Plato's Republic.

7. 'The unit of thought is a judgment; the unit of speech is a proposition.'

8. 'Nec ad rationem sed ad similitudinem vivimus.' Illustrate this from the practice of civilised nations.

LIII.

1. Mention the most important tyrannies that arose in the Grecian world before B.C. 400. Did the earlier tyrannies in any way contribute to the political development of Greece?

2. Compare the resources of Rome and Carthage at the beginning of the Punic Wars, indicating the special strength and weakness of each power. What is known of the constitution of Carthage?

3. Give a short account of the financial arrangements of the Roman empire in the first century of the Christian era.

4. Illustrate and criticise the following statements:

    (a) ὠνητὴ ἡ Ἀθηναίων δύναμις μᾶλλον ἢ οἰκεία.
    (b) ἐσώζοντο μὲν πολεμοῦντες, ἀπώλλοντο δὲ ἄρξαντες οἱ Λάκωνες.
    (c) Cn. Pompeius suarum legum auctor idem ac subversor, quæ armis tuebatur, armis amisit.
    (d) Latifundia perdidere Italiam.

5. In what respect may Greek tragedy be said to have reached its perfection in Sophocles? Illustrate from his dramas (1) his piety, (2) his irony, (3) his love of Homer.

6. Indicate the most striking peculiarities in the language and versification of Lucretius. Mention any Greek philosophical poems which may have served to some extent as models for his work, 'De Rerum Natura.'

LIV.

1. Give some account of the Great Revolution of 1688, and its results.

2. The advantages and disadvantages of vote by ballot.

3. Define the following phrases:

    A myth—a legend—an epic—a proverb—a

parable — an allegory — euphuism — euphemism.

4. Estimate the merits of any one of the three following historians: Lord Macaulay, Tacitus, Thucydides.

5. It has been said that 'mythology is diseased language.' Discuss this.

6. Explain and, if need, criticise:

    (*a*) Affirmantis est probare.
    (*b*) Good in theory, but bad in practice.
    (*c*) Parallels rarely run on all-fours.
    (*d*) Metaphors are not reasons.—*Bentham.*
    (*e*) He can't be wrong whose life is in the right.
                                         Pope.
    (*f*) Truth is the daughter of Time, rather than of Authority.—*Bacon.*

7. The causes of the decline of Turkish rule in Europe.

LV.

1. What was the influence of Persia upon the Peloponnesian War?

2. The origin and development of the plebeian tribunate at Rome.

3. Did the French revolutionists do well in regarding Brutus as a democratic martyr?

4. A brief sketch of the Roman policy towards Greece from the First Punic War to the end of the Republic.

5. What is meant by the Holy Roman Empire? What were its relations towards the See of Rome?

6. A short account of the First Crusade.

7. What was an Amphictyony? What instances of

it can you mention in Greece, and what was their political importance?

8. Explain the historical allusions in:

    (*a*) Unus homo nobis cunctando restituit rem.

    (*b*) Nihil aliud quam bene ausus vana contemnere.

    (*c*) Bedriaci in campo spolium adfectare Palati.

    (*d*) Hospes numinis Idæi.

    (*e*) Quid debeas o Roma Neronibus
Testis Metaurum flumen.

    (*f*) Think of him whom butchers murdered
On the field of Magus Muir.

    (*g*) Who filled the butchers' shops with large blue flies?

    (*h*) Or turns young Ammon loose to scourge mankind.

    (*i*) Fair Austria spreads her mournful charms;
The queen, the beauty, sets the world in arms.

9. The objects and importance of the League of Cambrai, the Holy Alliance, the League of the Fronde, the Constitutions of Clarendon, the Second Prayer-Book of King Edward VI.

10. Who were Mahmoud of Ghizni, Titus Oates, Abderrahman, Surajah Dowlah, Richelieu, Ivan the Terrible, Don John of Austria, Count Horn, Bernadotte, Hildebrand?

11. What induced (1) Spenser, (2) Chatterton, to write archaically?

12. In what sense is Pope a correct poet?

LVI.

1. Contrast the position of women in ancient Athens, in mediæval Europe, and in England of the present day.

2. State the chief legislative changes in England in the reign of Charles II.

3. What bearing has the science of language upon general historical study?

4. Compare Spanish and English colonisation in the New World, having regard to their respective purposes and results.

5. Describe the effects produced upon literature by the art of printing.

6. In what way did Savonarola, Loyola, and Wesley respectively affect the history of their times?

7. Why did the Romans fail in tragedy?

8. Describe briefly the establishment of Dutch independence in the sixteenth century, and estimate the permanent effects of the struggle upon European history.

9. Explain the policy of Argos in the Persian and Peloponnesian wars.

10. Give some account of the equestrian order at Rome.

11. Characterise the constitution of the kingdom of Judah. In what respects, and by what agencies, was the monarchy controlled?

LVII.

1. The importance of colonies, and their relation to the mother-country, in ancient and modern times.

2. The merits and defects of the Latin language compared with the Greek.

3. Explain fully what is meant by the 'synthetic' and 'analytic' stages of a language. Are they different stages, or only processes of the same stage?

4. Sketch any one or more of the female characters of Shakespeare.

5. The use of novels.

6. The meaning and value of Comparative Mythology.

7. Compare the feeling of the ancients for natural scenery with that of our own time.

8. Characteristics of any one great poet of the last three centuries.

9. Explain and discuss the following conceptions:

    (*a*) 'L'état c'est moi.'
    (*b*) 'Italy is only a geographical expression.'
    (*c*) 'History is an old almanack.'
    (*d*) 'La solidarité.'
    (*e*) 'Exceptio probat regulam.'
    (*f*) 'Materialism,' 'Pantheism,' 'Rationalism.'

10. What is meant by common sense? Is it always an adequate guide?

11. Explain the theory of 'Evolution,' and of 'Natural Selection.'

12. What evidence is there for the comparative age of geological formations?

LVIII.

1. The early races and languages of Italy.

2. 'In her days every man shall eat in safety
    Under his own vine what he plants, and sing
    The merry songs of peace to all his neighbours.'

Illustrate this characteristic of Queen Elizabeth's reign, as marking an epoch in English history.

3. The causes of the First French Revolution.

4. Trace the course of the principal rivers on the European continent, assigning both the ancient and modern names to the mountains, rivers, and seas which you mention.

5. The principal events which occurred between the accession of Charles I. and the commencement of the Civil War.

6. State the ordinary sequence of political phenomena in a Greek state, with illustrations.

7. Causes of the connection between Greece and Egypt in the sixth century, B.C.

8. What defence may be offered for the institutions of Sortition and Ostracism at Athens? To what are they analogous in our own history?

9. Give a particular account of the legislation of Solon. What questions, moral and economic, does it involve? Illustrate your solution of them from ancient or modern history.

LIX.

1. Give an account (with dates, if possible) of not more than two in each of the following classes:

> (*a*) Cleisthenes, Herodotus, Epaminondas, Philip of Macedon, Antiochus the Great.
> (*b*) Scipio Africanus, Sulla, Horace, Agricola, Constantine the Great.
> (*c*) Mahomet, Hugh Capet, Frederick Barbarossa, Dante, Erasmus, Don John of Austria.

(*d*) Bede, Lanfranc, the Black Prince, Warwick the Kingmaker, Lord Clarendon, Marlborough, the Old Pretender, John Wilkes, Washington.

2. Compare the influence of individuals on Athenian and Spartan history.

3. What information do we gain from the speeches of Demosthenes respecting the social state of Athens in his time?

4. Trace either (1) The rise of the Plebeians at Rome as a power in the state up to the First Punic War; or (2) the growth of the popular party in the last century of the Roman republic.

5. What were the occasions and causes of (1) the Great Rebellion in England? (2) The American War of Independence?

6. The immediate effects on Europe of the discoveries (1) of the passage round the Cape of Good Hope; (2) of America.

7. The extent of the empire of Charlemagne, and the causes that led to its dissolution.

8. The permanent effects on English history of the Wars of the Roses.

LX.

1. The influence of Egypt and Phœnicia on Jewish character and history.

2. What geographical characteristics of their country appear to have exercised the greatest influence on the history of the Greeks?

3. The political sympathies of Æschylus and Sophocles.

4. Sketch the rise of the Macedonian power in the time of Philip and Alexander.

5. Estimate Cicero as a statesman.

6. In what respects was the state of the world at the time of the introduction of Christianity favourable or otherwise to its diffusion?

7. Give an account of the historical events connected with any of the following places—Miletus, Syracuse, Capua, Alexandria, Ravenna, Avignon, Cologne, Genoa.

8. Give some account of any of the following—Simon de Montfort, Charles the Bold, Erasmus, Cranmer, Lord Burghley, Lord Strafford, Chatham, Canning.

9. Give a general sketch of the state of Europe at the time of either—

(1) The invasion of Italy by Charles VIII.
(2) The accession of William III. of England.

LXI.

1. The origin and history of the following words: Gentleman, cabal, Utopia, Whig, Tory, casuistry, sophistry, Puritanism, Romanticism.

2. Give some account of the writings and influence in English poetry of any two of the following: Chaucer, Spenser, Milton, Pope, Wordsworth.

3. Discuss any one of the following characters in Shakespeare: Richard II., Wolsey, Macbeth.

4. What is the meaning of: analogy, axiom, analysis, synthesis, metaphor, simile, species, balance of power, comparative philology, natural selection, argumentum ad hominem; 'there cannot be an unjust law;' 'the greater the truth, the greater the libel.'

5. Paraphrase in English prose:

> If it were done when 'tis done, then 'twere well
> It were done quickly: if the assassination
> Could trammel up the consequence, and catch
> With his surcease success; that but this blow
> Might be the be-all and the end-all here;
> But here, upon this bank and shoal of time,
> We'ld jump the life to come. But in these cases
> We still have judgment here; that we but teach
> Bloody instructions, which, being taught, return
> To plague the inventor: this even-handed justice
> Commends the ingredients of our poison'd chalice
> To our own lips.

LXII.

1. What views have been held concerning the date, composition, and mode of preservation of the Homeric poems?

2. Name the chief settlements of the Phœnicians, and give a sketch of the extent and character of their enterprise.

3. Contrast the influence of mountains, rivers, and seacoast on the development of national civilisation.

4. Draw characters of any *two* of the following persons, justifying your estimate of them by reference to history: Themistocles, Cicero, Marcus Aurelius, Savonarola, Henry VIII., Francis Bacon, Marlborough, Warren Hastings, Robespierre.

5. Give a brief account of (1) the Athenian expedition to Syracuse, or (2) the insurrection in Spain under Q. Sertorius.

6. How did the Carlovingian dynasty rise to sovereignty, and for what period did they retain it? How far did the dominion of Charlemagne extend at the time of his death?

7. Give the approximate dates of the principal Crusades, describing briefly the distinctive features of any which you remember.

8. Give a sketch of the progress of ecclesiastical architecture in England from A.D. 1100 to A.D. 1400.

9. For what reasons does a state punish offenders against its laws? Why does it not reward those who do right, as well as punish those who do wrong?

10. What events do you connect with the following places—Mantinea, Cannæ, Bedriacum, Senlac, Canossa, Worms, Barcelona, Saratoga? Give dates.

11. Contrast the present relation of the sovereign to the ministry and to Parliament, with that which existed in the reign of Anne.

12. Describe the northern frontier of India, and the possible routes by which an invading army could approach from Russia.

13. Give a short account of the writings of Pope, and add your own estimate of his genius.

14. Sketch the characteristics of English poetry since Wordsworth.

15. Under what circumstances, if any, is the imposition of export duties justifiable?

LXIII.

1. Estimate the prospects of Xerxes in 480 B.C. What were the causes of his failure?

2. What have been the effects of the Reformation on the character and European policy of the Papacy?

3. Illustrate from the history and literature of Greece the different characteristics of the Dorian and Ionian races.

4. What is meant by 'senatorial government' at Rome?

5. The origin of chivalry.

6. Explain briefly: 'free trade,' 'federal government,' 'equity.'

7. Draw a parallel between Ximenes and Richelieu.

LXIV.

1. Account for the frequency of the practice of historical 'rehabilitation.'

2. In what respects did the Byzantine empire present the characteristics of a Western, in what of an Oriental community?

3. Note and comment on the most remarkable occasions on which Christianity has been directly propagated by the sword.

4. Describe the political and social condition of England under Edward the Confessor.

5. Sketch the growth of monarchical power in France during the reigns of Philip Augustus, Philip the Fair, and Lewis XI.

6. Give some account of the most distinguished mediæval travellers, and of the extent of country which each visited.

7. Estimate and exemplify the military genius of Belisarius, Cromwell, and the Archduke Charles.

8. How far do the ecclesiastical peculiarities of Henry VIII.'s reign find a counterpart in Germany at the present time?

9. On what grounds, and with what propriety, has Queen Anne's reign been called, 'the Augustan age of English literature'?

10. What were the chief causes of the rise of British dominion in India?

11. Contrast the position of the Papacy in the middle of the sixteenth and of the eighteenth centuries.

12. Sketch the character and aims of Hincmar, Rienzi, Gerson, Bismarck, John Knox, Rousseau.

LXV.

1. 'Qui mari potitur is rerum potitur.' Illustrate historically.

2. The comparative importance under different circumstances of soldiers of different arms.

3. Compare the religions of early Greece and Italy.

4. Give a history of Roman satire.

5. Discuss the origin of the Greek sentiment as to the games at Olympia and elsewhere, and compare it with that of the Middle Ages as to tournaments.

6. How far has the sanction of Roman and English law been given to the judicial use of torture? Has practice agreed with theory in the matter?

7. The importance of the southern seaboard of the Mediterranean to the Roman empire.

8. What do you know of Giotto, Leibnitz, Addison, Erasmus, Akbar, Machiavelli, Suwarrow, Hofer, Euler, Colbert?

LXVI.

1. When is knowledge said to be superficial?
2. Does Art go beyond the imitation of Nature?
3. Sketch briefly the principal epochs in architecture.
4. An outline of the history of modern music.
5. Why are some occupations thought more or less honourable than others?
6. Is there necessarily a contrast between poetry and actual life?
7. State briefly the aspects of any one great question of the present time.
8. What do we mean by calling an author 'classical'?
9. Compare any two English poets, or one English with one foreign poet.
10. What causes make any article cheap or dear?
11. What agencies have produced geological changes?
12. The order of the principal discoveries in electrical science.
13. Will any considerations justify us in calling anything incredible which is supported by good evidence?

LXVII.

1. Contrast the state of society described in the 'Iliad' and 'Odyssey' with either (1) the patriarchal life described in the Old Testament, or (2) Greek society in the fifth century B.C.
2. How far can the following statement be supported by historical facts?

'In the youth of a state arms do flourish; in the middle age of a state, learning; and then both of them together for a time; in the declining age of a state, mechanical arts and merchandise.'

3. Show the influence of geographical situation on the history of Alexandria, Byzantium, Corinth, Venice.

4. The extent of the Roman empire at the time of the first diffusion of Christianity. What parts of it were visited by St. Paul?

5. Write an account of any two of the following, selecting, if possible, one subject from ancient and one from modern history:—

  (*a*) The life and political career of Demosthenes.
  (*b*) The war of Rome with Jugurtha.
  (*c*) The life and character of Marcus Aurelius Antoninus.
  (*d*) The Sicilian Vespers.
  (*e*) The Massacre of St. Bartholomew.
  (*f*) The reign of Elizabeth.

6. Give a short account of the more prominent English statesmen at either of the following periods:—

  (*a*) The reign of Charles I.
  (*b*) The time of the French Revolution.

7. Trace the growth of the dominions of the House of Austria.

LXVIII.

1. Illustrate from Greek history the advantages and disadvantages of the Spartan constitution.

2. Estimate the forces at work for the consolidation of the Greek race, and the causes which interfered with them.

3. Show how Themistocles, Cimon, Pericles, Thrasybulus were respectively typical representatives of different policies.

4. Give concisely the arguments an Athenian might have used to justify the conduct of Athens in its relations to its allies.

5. The nature of the 'ager publicus,' and the struggles to which it gave rise.

6. The character and functions of the different comitia at Rome.

7. What were the objects sought in the Social War, and the actual results of it?

8. Trace the importance of the history of women in the political history of Imperial Rome.

9. The principal events in the history of Russia.

LXIX.

1. State and explain the changes in the style and titles of our sovereigns since the sixteenth century.

2. Compare and contrast the enthusiasm of Mahomet, of Loyola, and of Cromwell.

3. What are the geographical difficulties of warfare in the Spanish peninsula? Give instances.

4. In what respect were Philip the Fair, Æneas Sylvius, Sir Walter Raleigh, and the younger Pitt, typical of the age in which each lived?

5. Contrast the general character of mediæval France north and south of the Loire; and account for the difference.

6. India has been described as the Italy of Asia. What historical grounds are there for such a comparison?

7. Give examples of sovereigns who have disappeared mysteriously; and discuss, in each case, the probabilities as to their fate.

8. Describe the administration of Thedoric the Ostrogoth, *or* of the Emperor Akbar.

9. Explain and exemplify the paradox that 'a country never knows its resources till it is ruined.'

10. Give some account of the most interesting crises of Turkish military history during the sixteenth and seventeenth centuries.

11. What were the most notable proceedings of the Councils of Clermont, Lyons, Constance, and Trent?

12. On what grounds, and with what propriety, were Louis XIV., the Czar Peter, and Frederick II. of Prussia called *The Great*?

LXX.

1. Write a Latin epitaph upon Livingstone.

2. Explain with reference to the history of literature the terms: 'précieuses,' 'troubadours,' 'minnesinger,' 'classicism,' 'euphuism.'

3. The chief causes and results of the American Civil War of 1861-5.

4. The causes of the success of the French arms in the wars which followed the Revolution.

5. What do you know of Cortes, Anne of Austria, Cyrus the Younger, the Great Condé, Baber, Mohammed of Ghuznee, Stigand?

6. Nicknames in history.

7. Why do schoolboys like to talk 'slang'?

8. Describe a day as spent by either (1) an Athenian gentleman in the time of Pericles, or (2) a Roman gentleman in the time of (*a*) Augustus, or (*b*) Domitian.

9. The chief centres of commerce in England at different epochs.

LXXI.

1. On what grounds do the classical languages remain the basis of education?

2. Ought the increase of national wealth to be an object to a statesman?

3. Discuss the reasons for which the state punishes criminals?

4. How far has a man right to do what he likes with his own?

5. What features are there in the poetry of the present century which are not found in ancient poetry?

6. What have been the principal causes of the spread of other religions than Christianity?

7. Sketch the social and political condition of Judæa and Samaria at the time of the birth of Christ.

8. State briefly the characteristics of Asceticism—Methodism—Calvinism—Materialism.

9. How has national art been influenced by scenery, or social conditions?

10. Give an account of any of the most marked epochs in the history of the Jewish monarchy.

LXXII.

1. Give a sketch of the careers of Camillus, Marius, and Pompey.

2. How did Athens rise to the leadership of Greece?

3. Give some account of the principal battles of the Peloponnesian War.

4. How did the Romans become masters of the following countries:—Sardinia—Transalpine Gaul—Judæa—Britain—Macedonia?

5. State your opinion of the murder of Julius Cæsar.

6. What events in French history furnish a parallel to the atrocities connected with the Paris Commune?

7. When were Florence, Genoa, Venice at the height of their prosperity? and what were the characteristics of each?

8. Give an outline of the history of the Long Parliament.

9. What have been the objects and success of sumptuary laws in ancient and modern times?

10. Whom do you consider the most illustrious English statesman since the Reformation?

LXXIII.

1. The place of the islands in Greek history.

2. What is meant by calling Athens the school of Hellas?

3. The history of the Roman tribunate.

4. Show that the Roman empire was the necessary result of the existing political condition.

5. What was Puritanism? Estimate its result on English history.

6. 'Poetry is essentially of the people and for the people.' Is this true?

LXXIV.

1. Comment on the following passages:

(*a*) I am but mad north-north-west: when the wind is southerly, I know a hawk from a handsaw.

(b)   Head to foot
Now is he total gules: horridly tricked
With blood of fathers, mothers, daughters, sons.

(c) He'll watch the horologe a double set,
If drink rock not his cradle.

(d) Up springen speres twenty foot on highte;
Out goon the swerdes as the silver brighte;
The helmes thei to-hewen and to-schrede;
Out brest the blood, with sterne stremes reede.

Explain the metre and any peculiar forms in the last passage.

2. What is the literary value of translations from the classics?

3. Write short notices with approximate dates of the lives and works of the following authors:—Marvell, Erasmus, Hobbes, Picus of Mirandola, Goldsmith, Burke, Defoe.

4. Give a brief account of the following works:— 'Cymbeline,' 'Areopagitica,' 'The Hind and the Panther,' 'The Essay on Man,' 'The Task.'

5. Compare the influence of various foreign literatures upon English literature at different periods.

6. Mention the principal English essay-writers, their works and their respective characteristics. Who was the originator of this style of writing?

7. How would you establish from internal evidence that Scott's poems and the Waverley novels were written by the same man?

8. Comment on the following passages with reference to the context, mentioning the name of the author in each case:

(1) The unbought grace of life, the cheap defence of nations, the nurse of manly sentiment and heroic enterprise is gone!

(2) The clouds that gather round the setting sun
Do take a sober colouring from an eye
That hath kept watch on man's mortality.

(3) The gods are just, and of our pleasant vices
Make instruments to scourge us.

(4) Fame is the spur that the clear spirit doth raise
(That last infirmity of noble minds)
To scorn delights and live laborious days.

(5) For we are ancients of the earth,
And in the morning of the times.

9. What were the causes which led to the literary and artistic eminence of Athens in the age of Pericles?

10. Give some account of Agesilaus, Epaminondas, Agathocles, Sertorius, Mithridates, Arminius.

11. Trace the rise of Prussia as a power in Europe.

12. What was the origin of the names Guelph and Ghibelline? Give some account of the struggles between these factions.

13. Contrast the general course of constitutional history in England, France and Germany.

LXXV.

1. What are the most important points in the history of the relations of Athens with other nations?

2. Explain the condition of Athenian politics in the time of Demosthenes.

3. Explain what was meant by an agrarian law, and state at what times such laws had the greatest influence on affairs in Rome.

4. Sketch the events in Roman history between the battles of Pharsalia and Actium.

5. Compare the Greek and Roman national character.

6. Explain what is meant by the terms 'dikastery,' 'Peripatetic,' 'proconsul,' 'humanist,' 'Frondeur,' 'Romanesque,' 'Commune.'

7. Contrast the aims of the Crusades with their results.

8. Describe any two of the following battles: Evesham, Flodden, Blenheim, Sedan.

9. What are the chief features of the reign of Elizabeth?

10. What were the causes of the rise of the first Napoleon?

11. The position of the Jews at the Reformation, and their connection with it.

LXXVI.

1. Illustrate the relation of physical geography to civilisation by reference to the inhabitants of (1) islands, (2) peninsulas, (3) central plains.

2. What laws or constitutional changes are associated with the names of Lycurgus, Cleisthenes, Licinius Stolo, and Sulla?

3. What is meant by 'comparative mythology'?

4. Give an account of three of the following persons: Cleon, Socrates, Appius Claudius Cæcus, Vespasian, Ignatius Loyola, Reginald Pole, Marlborough, Washington.

5. Describe the course of the Elbe, naming the chief towns situated upon it, and show its importance in war.

6. Where are Nicæa, Canossa, Clermont, Pavia, Glencoe, Londonderry, Vittoria? With what famous events are they connected?

7. Describe the policy of William the Conqueror towards the English and Normans respectively.

8. Describe and criticize the characters of Hamlet and Lady Macbeth.

9. Does 'Robinson Crusoe' fulfil the conditions of a fiction?

10. Point out the influence of domestic and other animals in affecting the habits and characters of races.

LXXVII.

1. Give a brief explanation of the following: Paradox, consciousness, personal identity, pessimism, temperament, centralisation, motive, fallacy, materialism, æsthetics.

2. When and on what grounds may a literary work be termed a classic?

3. 'Omnes homines naturâ æquales sunt.'
  'Naturæ non nisi parendo imperatur.'
Comment briefly on these maxims.

4. 'Mountains divide, and rivers unite, nations.'
Discuss this assertion.

5. Give a critical estimate of any one of the following:—Spenser, Cowley, Dryden, Burns, Shelley.

6. 'History is the complement of poetry, and poetry is the complement of history.' Explain and illustrate.

7. 'The victory over sin and death is with the Greek tragedians more complete than with Shakespeare.' Examine this statement.

LXXVIII.

1. Contrast the political effects of a standing army and a militia.

2. Illustrate the danger of mixing romance with history.

3. To what extent is it desirable that the State should encourage emigration?

4. Summarize the distinctive peculiarities of the following literary epochs: age of Elizabeth, of the Civil Wars, of Anne.

5. Discuss the applications of science to military operations.

LXXIX.

1. Ancient history has been said to differ from modern only in time. Point out (briefly) other important differences.

2. 'The rise, or increase, of great powers has been the result of some new discovery in tactics or weapons.' Illustrate this.

3. Compare the power of the Ephors at Sparta with that of the Tribunes at Rome.

4. Characters of Phocion, Nicias, Scipio Africanus, Nero, Seneca.

5. What is a limited monarchy? Sketch the methods adopted for the maintenance of such a system in Spain, England, Germany, and France; and measure their success.

6. Enumerate the chief religious and political questions which led to the rebellion against Charles I., and distinguish the several parties into which the anti-royal party broke up.

7. Compare the political position of Francis I. with that of Henry IV. in reference (1) to the house of Austria, (2) to the position of France in European politics.

8. Give some account of the ways in which English fleets and armies were formed during the Middle Ages.

9. Enumerate the principal English cardinals, and distinguish them as to personal and political importance.

10. The life and genius of Rabelais.

LXXX.

1. Examine the causes which led to the Peloponnesian War.

2. Give some account of four of the following persons: Tiberius Gracchus, Aristarchus, Herod Antipas, Augustine of Hippo, Dante, Francis Bacon, Ulfilas, Pascal, Giotto, Beethoven, Mazzini.

3. Describe: (1) the extent and character of the empire of Solomon; (2) the life and writings of Isaiah.

4. The likeness and difference between poetry and the other arts.

5. Draw a map of the Black Sea, with the approaches from the Archipelago, marking all the important places and the mouths of the rivers, with the ancient and modern names.

6. Contrast the view taken of slavery in ancient and modern times.

7. Give an account of any one of the Crusades. How far were they successful in their object, and what indirect consequences followed from them?

8. Describe the immediate and the permanent effects of the Norman conquest of England.

9. Contrast the types of national character exhibited by the Greeks and Romans.

10. Give some account of the chief Roman historians and their writings.

11. Εὐφυοῦς ἡ ποιητική ἐστιν ἢ μανικοῦ· τούτων γὰρ οἱ μὲν εὔπλαστοι οἱ δὲ ἐκστατικοί εἰσιν. Consider these words.

12. With what fitness does Plutarch compare the lives of Demosthenes and Cicero?

13. The effect of (1) the Persian invasion, or (2) the conquests of Alexander, or (3) the conquests of the Saracens.

14. Trace the principal watersheds and river-basins of Great Britain, and describe minutely the one with which you are best acquainted.

LXXXI.

1. How do you rate English among languages ancient and modern as to (1) copiousness of vocabulary, (2) facility of expression? State clearly the facts upon which you base your answer.

2. Show how the every-day life of the Athenian is reflected in the metaphors of the dramatists and orators.

3. Compare Æschylus and Sophocles as to (1) the dramatic machinery employed by each, (2) the treatment of the mythical stories which they handled.

4. Illustrate from 'Hamlet' the care with which Shakespeare discriminates his minor characters.

5. What are the chief points of a good historical style? Answer chiefly by referring to Greek and Latin historians. Do you consider that Cicero was well qualified to write history?

6. A man had killed another at Athens. Describe his trial.

7. Illustrate the strong and weak points in the Athenian empire.

8. Describe the attempts made by different Greek states to resist the advance of the power of Macedon.

9. The causes, history, and results of the different secessions at Rome.

10. The policy and character of Tiberius.

11. Describe the different elements contributed to the English Reformation by the reigns of Henry VIII., Edward VI., and Elizabeth.

12. Write characters of Anselm, Pym, and William III.

13. What is meant by the 'balance of power in Europe?' What wars have been at any time carried on to secure it?

LXXXII.

1. 'A little knowledge is a dangerous thing.' Explain this.

2. Why should a man keep his word?

3. Sketch the objects and results of the Council of Constance.

4. Explain the following:

    (*a*) An inductive process.

(b) It is difficult to prove a negative.
(c) The exception proves the rule.
(d) No rule is without an exception.

5. What differences are there between Athenian and English tragedy, and how can they be accounted for?

6. Give the most memorable names and incidents connected with the Gens Claudia.

7. Give some account of Pericles, Nicias, Pope Gregory VII., the Emperor Joseph II., Gustavus Adolphus.

8. Discuss the following aphorisms:
(a) Antiquitas sæculi juventus mundi.
(b) Naturæ non imperatur nisi parendo.
(c) Vox populi vox Dei.

9. What was the Confederacy of Delos, and what important results sprang from it?

10. 'Metaphors reflect the life of a people.' Explain and illustrate this.

LXXXIII.

1. What questions other than religious were at issue in the Thirty Years' War, and how were they ultimately decided?

2. What were the causes of the supremacy of Spain under Philip II., and what were the reasons of her subsequent decline?

3. Explain the long resistance of the Byzantine Empire to the attacks of its enemies.

4. What were the irremediable defects of the Crusades as military expeditions?

5. What were the circumstances which facilitated the spread of the Reformation in Germany?

LXXXIV.

1. What were the economical results of:
    - (a) The Black Death;
    - (b) The Wars of the Roses;
    - (c) The Reformation?

2. Account for the Roman Catholic reaction under Mary.

3. Illustrate the influence of the Norman Conquest and the Hundred Years' (French) War on the relations of England and Scotland.

4. What is Clarendon's account of the temper and condition of the country? How far is it consistent with fact?

5. Give an account of the following, showing their influence on the course of affairs:—
    - (a) Goring's Plot.
    - (b) The Bishops' Protest.
    - (c) Waller's Plot.

LXXXV.

1. Explain the meaning of the following terms:
    - (a) 'Cujus regio ejus religio.'
    - (b) 'Ecclesiastical reservation.'
    - (c) 'Royal Charter of Bohemia.'

2. What events tended to check the growth of the royal power in France from the reign of Charles VIII. to the death of Henry IV.?

3. 'It was Martin V. who sowed the seed of modern Ultramontanism.' Examine this statement.

4. State and account for the variety in the deve-

lopment of Feudalism in England, France, and Germany.

5. Give the characteristic differences of the popular institutions of France and England; and explain the causes of their success and failure in the different countries.

LXXXVI.

1. 'The general features of the Tudors coincided, those of the Stuarts conflicted, with the wants and aspirations of their people. Hence the success of the former, the failure of the latter.' Explain and illustrate.

2. Explain briefly the judicial system of the Anglo-Saxons, and show how it was modified by the reforms of Henry I. and Henry II.

3. Contrast the foreign policy of Edward I. and Edward III.

4. Sketch the history of military organisation from the Norman Conquest to the reign of Henry VIII.

5. Show how and why the attitude of the Church to the Crown was altered at the accession of the Lancastrian kings, and briefly state the results of that change.

6. Trace the growth of English nationality up to the reign of Edward I., pointing out the causes which contributed to it at the several decisive epochs.

7. Sketch the course of the quarrel between the English kings and the Pope from the reign of William I. to that of John.

8. Account for the fact that Wessex was the last to gain the supremacy of England, and that she permanently maintained it.

LXXXVII.

1. Give an account of the rise of the kingdom of Prussia.

2. Account for the fact that the monarchical principle of government was less commonly accepted by Greek and Roman communities than in modern states.

3. Show how various provinces of the Roman empire successively took the lead in literary activity; and compare in this respect the history of modern Europe.

4. The origin and principal incidents of the struggle of the Guelphs and Ghibellines.

5. Is the writing of novels to be considered a branch of the Fine Arts?

6. The causes of the English Revolution of 1688.

7. In what circumstances may free trade, whether between one state and another, or within a state, be undesirable?

8. The causes of the stability of the Swiss republic.

9. The tendency of the legislation of the reigns of Edward I. and George IV.

10. The permanent results upon history of the public life of (1) Cleisthenes, (2) Epaminondas, (3) Sulla, (4) Louis XIV., (5) Calvin, (6) Penn, (7) the first Lord Nottingham.

11. Give an account of the following books: The Castle of Indolence—Areopagitica—The Anti-Jacobin—Hyperion—Pascal's Provincial Letters—Goethe's Faust.

12. Explain the expressions: Instinct, Cause, Republican, Political Economy, Civilisation.

LXXXVIII.

1. Specify the Greek colonies in the West previous to the Peloponnesian War, and give facts to show the relations subsisting between them and their mother states.

2. What reasons can be given for the decline of the Senate towards the close of the Roman Republic?

3. What were the principal reforms attempted by Augustus? Illustrate from the authors of his time.

4. Write the life and character of Alcibiades, *or* Agesilaus.

5. Describe the battle of Pharsalia, *or* Platæa.

6. Give an account of the reign of Henry II. of England.

7. Exemplify and explain the want of harmony between Parliament and popular sentiment in England during the eighteenth century.

8. Sketch the history of the Low Countries from the beginning of the sixteenth century to the present day.

LXXXIX.

1. Paraphrase and explain:

' As the Births of Living Creatures at first are ill-shapen, so are all *Innovations* which are the Births of Time; yet notwithstanding, as those that first bring Honour into their Family are commonly more worthy than most that succeed; so the first Precedent (if it be good) is seldom attained by Imitation. For Ill to Man's Nature, as it stands perverted, hath a natural Motion, strongest in continuance; but Good, as a forced Motion, strongest at first. Surely every *Medicine* is an *Innovation*; and he that will not apply new Remedies must expect new Evils;

for Time is the greatest *Innovator*: and if Time of course alter Things to the worse, and Wisdom and Counsel shall not alter them to the better, what shall be the End?'

2. The comparative dignity of the lives of the politician and the philosopher.

3. What are the fundamental differences between poetry and prose?

4. Explain the following terms: Purism, Romanticism, Classicism, Mixed Government, Natural Right, Three Estates of the Realm.

5. Ἀρχὴ θαλάττης ἀρχὴ κακῶν. The advantages and the drawbacks of naval supremacy.

6. Compare the ancient languages with the modern as instruments of education.

7. 'Malo cum Platone errare quam cum istis vera sentire.' Criticise this doctrine.

XC.

1. The moral and political effects on Greece of the defeat of Xerxes.

2. Mention the chief colonies to the west of Greece, with the probable dates of the foundation of each. What share had any of them in Greek history?

3. The parties to, and the provisions of, the more important treaties of Greek history.

4. The more prominent points of contrast between Athenian and Roman character.

5. Compare the Roman system of provincial government with that of the distant dependencies of this country.

6. What events happened at the following places: Lade, Delium, Chæronea, Cynocephalæ, Zama, Vercellæ, the Colline Gate, Pharsalus.

7. Sketch the ordinary career of a Roman noble in the best times of the Republic.

8. Sketch the character of any *two* of the following: Cimon, Xenophon, Epaminondas, Æschines, Fabius Maximus, Jugurtha, Cicero, the Emperor Claudius, William I., Wolsey, James I., Charles the Bold.

9. How far is it possible to trace a common character in each of the dynasties of English sovereigns since the Conquest?

10. The beneficial effects of the Crusades upon European civilisation.

XCI.

1. The use and abuse of manuals in education.

2. Comment *briefly* on the following: sovereignty—museum—ecstasy—idiot—cavalier—cant—apology—prejudice.

3. Mention your favourite prose writer, with a brief account of him, and the grounds of your selection.

4. Is the existence of a permanent standard of beauty compatible with variations of taste?

5. The real political dangers of the future in

   (1) Western Europe.
   (2) North America.

6. Describe the character indicated by the word 'dilettante,' and examine the justice of the depreciatory impression which it conveys.

XCII.

1. Give some account of the Troubadours in connection with the places and times in which they flourished.

2. Compare the feudal aristocracy with the aristocracies of classical antiquity.

3. Write a brief plea and counter-plea upon the character of Julius Cæsar.

4. Trace chronologically the rise of successive states to leadership in ancient Greece.

5. Give a short description of the geography of the Peloponnesus, *or* of India, *or* of Lombardy.

6. Examine the claims of the Plantagenet monarchs to be considered, on the whole, *intellectually* eminent.

7. Give some account of the rise and progress of *the Novel* in England.

8. Sketch the more prominent characteristics of *either* the Renaissance, *or* Scholasticism, *or* the age of Louis XIV.

9. What is meant by *Constitutional* History? Illustrate your answer by any *one* English reign.

10. Compare the military genius of Cromwell, Marlborough, Napoleon.

11. Describe and account for the part played in European history by *either* Venice, *or* Holland, *or* Poland.

12. At what periods, since the accession of Henry VII., has the prestige of England as a European power been at its lowest; and why?

13. Assign to any *two* of the following their place in history: Rienzi, Philip II. of Spain, Richelieu, Canning, James I. of England, Peter the Great, Cavour.

14. What are the principal changes in the political map of Europe since the battle of Pavia?

XCIII.

1. Contrast the political effects of a standing army and a militia.

2. Illustrate the danger of mixing romance with history.

3. Indicate briefly the various phases through which the struggle for freedom in our own country has passed since the end of the sixteenth century.

4. Examine the ideas conveyed by these words: γνώμη, 'sentiment,' 'maxim,' 'proverb.'

5. The geography of Latium, and its bearing upon the early history of Rome.

6. Under what limitations should a state encourage emigration?

7. What is the essential difference between an ancient tragedy and a modern oratorio, or between an ancient and a modern comedy?

8. The position of Athens as conceived by Pericles. To what dangers was his policy exposed?

9. Compare the characters of Clytæmnestra in the 'Agamemnon' and Lady Macbeth, or those of the Œdipus of Sophocles and King Lear.

10. What was Stoicism as seen in Cicero, Juvenal, or Persius?

11. What influences tended to arrest the decline and fall of the Roman Empire?

12. Describe and compare the political aims of Cicero and Demosthenes.

XCIV.

1. Are there any indications in ancient history of the balance of power being recognised as a political principle?

2. Under what conditions would it be possible to establish a system of international law? How far have those conditions ever been actually realised?

3. Criticise the claims of Herodotus to be considered scientific, philosophic, or artistic in his treatment of history.

4. 'Ye men of Athens, I perceive that in all things ye are too superstitious.' Illustrate this statement from Greek literature and from history, and examine its truth.

5. Sketch the life and character of Alcibiades. May he be looked upon as a representative Athenian?

6. Point out the causes and characteristics of Roman cosmopolitanism.

7. What were the merits and defects of the Sullan constitution?

8. 'Arcana imperii.' Specify the leading features of the imperial system. To what extent had they been foreshadowed in the democratic programme?

9. Trace the steps in the emancipation of women at Rome.

XCV.

1. What are Hume's views on the questions of Church establishment, free-trade, monastic institutions, and the origin of the Reformation?

2. Explain the terms: Communism, Socialism, Radicalism, Nihilism.

3. Write a brief account of—Prince Bismarck, Talleyrand, O'Connell, Cobden, Cavour.

4. Estimate the character and career of Alexander the Great.

5. State reasons for the greater abundance of metaphors in Latin than in Greek.

6. Compare Pindar's treatment of legends with that of the tragedians.

7. Give some account of philological studies among the Romans as evidenced by extant works.

8. Discuss the origin of pastoral poetry, its legitimate scope, and its treatment by Greek and Roman authors.

9. The qualifications of a literary critic.

10. To what causes do you attribute the decline of sculpture?

11. How far is there a common character underlying the various forms of comedy?

XCVI.

1. Compare the position of Rome and Carthage at the opening of the Second Punic War. Indicate the chief points of strength and weakness on the part of each.

2. Give an account of the condition of Athens, Sparta, and Thebes at the time of the death of Philip of Macedon.

3. What was the real issue involved in the struggle between Pompey and Julius Cæsar? What amount of strength did the support of the Senate give to the former?

4. What circumstances in the conversion of the barbarians to Christianity contributed to the growth of the power of the Popes?

5. Give a brief account of the circumstances which led to, and gave its peculiar character to the Revolution of 1688.

6. Mark carefully the several alterations in the political map of Europe which have been made since the treaties of 1814–1815.

7. Consider the meaning and value of the following sayings :—'Extremes meet.' 'No man is a hero to his own valet.' 'Might is right.' 'De mortuis nil nisi bonum.'

XCVII.

1. Illustrate the extent of Greek commerce.
2. Why did Greece outstrip Oriental nations in art.
3. Compare the magistracies of Athens and Rome.
4. Which do you consider the five great battles of Roman history, and why?
5. The transition from democracy to imperialism at Rome.
6. Illustrate the history of English commerce from the rise and decline of ports.
7. The prerogatives of the Crown under the Tudors and the Hanoverians.
8. Reasons for the predominance and decline of Spain.
9. The main revolutions in military tactics during the last three centuries.
10. The political bearings and connections of Protestantism during the sixteenth and seventeenth centuries.
11. Who were Locke, Reid, Berkeley? Explain the following terms: Metaphysical, Utilitarian, Phenomenal, Unconditioned.
12. Explain: the Scholiasts, the Lake Poets, Corinthian Capital, La Fronde, Anti-Jacobin, Peter Pindar, Girondist, Lollard, Les Gueux, Falk Laws, Maine Liquor Law.

XCVIII.

1. Discuss Lord Macaulay's claims as a poet, an essayist, or an historian.

2. Trace the connection between the religion and the national character of England.

3. Point out the limits of voluntary almsgiving.

4. The character and policy of any of these German emperors: Barbarossa, Frederic II., Charles V., Maria Theresa.

5. What arguments are there in favour of railways being purchased by the State?

6. Should barristers have a legal claim to be paid for their services?

7. The chief causes of the decadence of either Spain or Turkey.

8. The chief modifications of English character in America.

9. What are the chief objections to anonymous writing?

10. On what principles should an imperial State govern dependencies?

11. Can the unselfish man cease to be self-regarding?

12. Give some account of 'The era of the British Essayists.'

XCIX.

1. What were the chief turning points in the Peloponnesian War?

2. Contrast the characters of Sulla and Cæsar.

3. Compare Rome and England in their treatment of subject States.

4. Sketch the campaigns of Hannibal in the Second Punic War.

5. Give some account of Greek 'tyranny' as illustrated by the lives of Periander, Pisistratus, and Hiero.

6. What were the main features in the public life of an Athenian in the time of Pericles?

7. 'The Holy Roman Empire.' Explain the kind of power implied by this phrase, and the chief holders of it.

8. Trace the gradual extension of the French monarchy.

9. The chief victories of Napoleon I.

10. A short account of any reforming movements before the Reformation.

11. The character and political aims of Cromwell.

12. 'George III. had a smaller mind than any English king before him, except James II.' Examine this statement.

C.

1. In what ways are literature and art affected by patronage?

2. Trace the effects of the French Revolution on the poetry of the present century.

3. By what causes was the issue of the Peloponnesian War mainly determined?

4. Illustrate, from authors you have read, life at Rome in the time of Augustus.

5. Trace the causes of the decline of cities, and their effect upon the development of a nation.

6. What is meant when the English monarchy is called limited? What are its most important limitations?

7. Mention some of the great battle-fields of Europe, and point out the physical features that have determined them.

8. What qualities must the works of a prose author or poet possess if they are to become classical?

9. Illustrate the social and political position of the Equites at Rome in the later Republic.

10. What were the real points at issue between Charles I. and his Parliament?

11. Mention any circumstances that mark the reign of Henry VIII. as one of transition from mediæval to modern history in politics, war, literature, enterprise, amusements, or domestic habits.

CI.

1. Mention, with examples, some of the more important objects of Greek colonisation.

2. What were the provisions of the Licinian laws, and how far did they effect the purpose for which they were framed?

3. What changes did Sulla make in the constitution of Rome?

4. Illustrate the importance of the army in the imperial times of Rome.

5. What were the grievances which led to the French Revolution?

6. Enumerate the chief characteristics of *any* orator either in ancient or modern times.

7. How far can the Æneid lay claim to originality?

8. Write a short critique of any one play of Shakespeare?

9. Sketch, in connection with their time, *any two* of the following:—Abelard, Dante, Isaac Casaubon, Milton, Voltaire.

CII.

1. Paraphrase and explain :—

' But *Good Conservative* is no other than *the reception and fruition of things agreeable to our Nature*; and this *Good* tho it bee most simple and Native; yet seems it to be of all other kinds of *Good* the softest and lowest, And this *Good* also admits of a difference, which hath neither bin well judg'd of, nor well inquired; for the *Good of Fruition*, or (as it is commonly called) the dignitie and commendation of *delightfull Good*, is placed either in the *Syncerity of the Fruition*, or in the *quicknesse and vigor* of it; whereof the one is superinduced by *Equality*; the other by *Variety* and *Vicissitude*: the one having a lesse mixture of *Evill*; the other a more strong and lively impression of *Good*. But of these *whether is the Greater Good,* is a question controverted; But *whether a man's nature may be capable of both at once is a question not inquired.*'

2. Discuss, with illustrations, the power and value of quotation.

3. 'Manners are stronger than laws.' Explain and illustrate this.

4. ' Piece out our imperfections with your thoughts.' The nature and necessity of dramatic illusion.

5. 'Grâces donc soient rendues à la nature pour les incompatibilités, pour les luttes de la vanité, pour la cupidité insatiable, même pour la passion de commander.' Show how these qualities contribute to human progress, and how far they are insufficient to account for it.

6. 'Perhaps there is no instance of any ancient writing proved to be a forgery, which combines great excellence with considerable length.' Examine this statement. Can it be applied to modern literature?

7. What are the various characteristics which contribute to the genius and popularity of Sir Walter Scott as a novelist?

CIII.

1. State the main features of the geography of Attica and Bœotia.

Did geographical differences lead to differences in the character and history of the Athenians and Bœotians?

2. What different views have been, or may be, taken of the Trojan War?

3. Describe the siege of Platæa, or the siege of Syracuse, in the Peloponnesian War.

4. Causes and effects of the increased number of mercenaries in Greece in the fourth century.

5. Compare the Greek phalanx and the Roman manipular legion in point of constitution and efficiency.

6. What were the causes of Hannibal's temporary success and ultimate failure in his invasion of Italy?

7. Do you agree with the detractors of Cicero?

8. Contrast the real and alleged causes of the French wars under Henry V.

9. Influence of the Norman invasion on English civilisation.

10. Characters of any two of the following:—Richard I., the Black Prince, Sir Philip Sidney, Laud, Atterbury, Burke.

CIV.

1. How far is political action to be judged by ordinary moral standards?

2. Can satire be fairly taken as an evidence of the social condition of an age?

3. Compare the position of a leading statesman of a Greek republic with that of a minister of a modern State.

4. Illustrate the growth of the sense of the picturesque.

5. Of what value is the encouragement to trade afforded by a taste for luxuries?

6. State briefly the forms in which Greece and Rome respectively have most influenced the thought and action of later ages.

7. How did Rome govern her dependencies?

8. Illustrate the different forms taken by colonial enterprise.

9. What kinds of poetry may be regarded as an expression of, or as a reaction against, the tendencies of their age?

10. Discuss briefly the origin and character of the feudal system.

CV.

1. What different meanings attach to the words Hellenism?

2. Illustrate by examples the growth of myths.

3. Write a brief life of Alexander of Macedon, *or* of Caius Gracchus.

4. What issues were at stake in the Peloponnesian War, *or* in the war between Cæsar and Pompey?

5. How far is patriotism a merely heathen virtue?

6. Write a brief life of Mahomet. Give the leading tenets of Islam, and compare their civilising force with that of Christianity.

7. What is meant by 'the balance of power'? Estimate its value as a political principle, and defend your opinions by historical evidence.

8. When have the conditions necessary for international law been most nearly realised?

9. Write a brief criticism of one of the following books:
    (*a*) Mill's 'Autobiography.'
    (*b*) Trevelyan's 'Life of Lord Macaulay.'
    (*c*) Newman's 'Apologia.'
    (*d*) Wordsworth's 'Excursion.'

10. What is meant by the Pagan Renaissance in literature?

11. 'The natural causes which led to the commercial prosperity of England are gradually ceasing to act, and her position is already artificial.' Criticise this statement.

CVI.

1. What were the causes of the predominance of Sparta in Greece?

2. Describe the origin and nature of the power of the Tribunes at Rome.

3. Give a brief history of the Reformation in England up to the death of Queen Elizabeth.

4. Write a short account of any three of the following: Cambyses, Cimon, Sulla, Lessing, Voltaire, Becket, Erasmus, Dryden.

5. 'The object of art is only to give pleasure.' Criticise this.

6. Define education, and show how physical education comes under your definition.

7. What are the principal nationalities of Europe, and how far do they correspond with the existing political divisions?

8. Examine the following statements:
   (*a*) Luxury is good for trade.
   (*b*) The exception proves the rule.
   (*c*) The end justifies the means.
   (*d*) A limited monarchy is a contradiction in terms.

9. Explain shortly the meaning of Tiers Etat, Mysticism, λειτουργίαι, Petition of Right, Commune, Ultramontane, Darwinism, Pre-Raphaelite.

CVII.

1. Write a character of Demosthenes as a statesman and an orator.

2. Was slavery more defensible in ancient than it is in modern times?

3. Describe and estimate the importance of one of the following battles: Salamis, Pydna, Naseby, and Blenheim.

4. The structure of the Apennine Mountains, and its influence on Italian history.

5. Trace the march of Xerxes, and point out the chief places where he might have been opposed.

6. Compare an Athenian with an English law court.

7. The influence of the Roman army on politics in the later times of the Republic.

8. 'War plays a small part in the real story of European nations.' Criticise this statement.

9. 'Runnymede reversed the decision of Hastings.' Comment upon this.

10. Give a character of Louis XI., and point out the importance of his reign in the history of France.

CVIII.

1. Paraphrase and explain:

'It cannot be denied, but Outward Accidents conduce much to Fortune: Favour, Opportunitie, Death of Others, Occasion fitting Vertue. But chiefly, the Mould of a Man's Fortune, is in his owne hands. Faber quisque Fortunæ suæ; saith the Poet. And the most Frequent of Externall Causes is, that the Folly of one Man, is the Fortune of Another. For no man prospers so suddenly, as by Others Errours. Serpens nisi Serpentem comederit non fit Draco. Overt, and Apparent Vertues bring forth praise; But there be Secret and Hidden Vertues that bring forth Fortune. Certaine Deliveries of a Man's Selfe, which have no Name. The Spanish Name, Desemboltura, partly expresseth them: when there be not Stonds, nor Restivenesse in a Man's Nature; But that the wheeles of his Minde keepe way, with the wheeles of his Fortune.'

2. Distinguish between change of opinion and inconsistency. Can you quote, from history, any instances in which they have been confused?

3. How far are the popular wishes a means of ensuring good legislation?

4. 'Tragedy is the miniature of human life.' Explain and criticise this statement.

5. Advantages and disadvantages of centralisation and decentralisation respectively.

6. Explain the following terms: Optimism, Pessimism ; Right, Freedom ; Egotism, Indifferentism ; Justice, Legality.

7. Describe the main currents of thought in contemporary poetry.

CIX.

1. Distinguish historically the meaning of the terms 'emperor,' 'tyrant,' 'democracy,' 'socialism.'

2. By what different standards may we measure the degrees of social progress?

3. Discuss the value of Stoicism as a moral creed.

4. Was there anything in ancient literature like the novel? Which of its features seem most modern?

5. Illustrate the moral influence of great plagues or revolutions.

6. What sort of help may we get from works of art, other than literary, towards understanding classical antiquity?

7. Specify with illustrations the chief qualifications of the historian.

8. Illustrate the sense of the picturesque in ancient writers. What elements in it seem most modern?

9. The history and the value of the chorus in the Greek drama, both tragic and comic.

10. The influence of rhetoric and of law upon Latin literature.

11. The literary inspiration, place, and influence of any of the following : Pindar, Xenophon, Callimachus, Ennius, Catullus, Quintilian.

12. Illustrate the meaning of the epithet Augustan, as applied to literature.

CX.

1. Show from any Latin authors the chief defects or vices of public life at Rome.

2. Give a sketch of the events that brought (1) Pericles, (2) Demosthenes, into the foremost place at Athens.

3. Compare the English and French Revolutions in their *results* only.

4. Explain the meaning of the following terms, with a careful statement of their origin: Romantic, Æsthetic, Ultramontane, Secular, Federalism, Imperialism, Lyrical.

5. Describe briefly the subjects, and give the authorship of the following treatises: Utopia, Rasselas, Religio Laici, The Areopagitica, The Novum Organum, The Letters of Phalaris.

6. Compare the literary styles of Gibbon and Macaulay.

7. How far can it be justly said that it is a painter's duty to paint precisely what he sees?

CXI.

1. Describe the geographical position and historical importance of Damascus, Tyre, Miletus, Corinth, Alexandria, Malta.

2. What issues were decided by the battles of Bethhoron, Leuctra, Metaurus, Quebec?

3. Illustrate the peculiar position and influence of the Spartan kings.

4. Compare the political careers of Demosthenes and Cicero.

Historical and General Questions.   93.

5. Give a brief historical sketch of the general relations of Italy to Rome until the death of Julius Cæsar.

6. Account historically for the present distribution of the races of Western Europe into Protestant and Catholic.

7. The past and present position of the Sovereign in the English constitution.

8. Are the obligations of international morality binding between all nations.

9. Discuss and illustrate the advantages and disadvantages of small and large estates.

10. Trace the influence of Mirabeau on the course of the French Revolution.

11. Give a sketch of Mahommedan conquest and civilisation in Europe.

CXII.

1. Write a short life of Alcibiades.

2. Show how the idea of νέμεσις affects Greek literature.

3. What explanation can be given of Hannibal's failure to attack Rome?

4. What do you know of the history of Byzantium before it became the capital of the Roman Empire?

5. State the benefits which may be considered as accruing to Europe from the Crusades.

6. Give some account of the political events which followed the extinction of the male line of Hapsburg in Spain and Austria.

7. Sketch the principal social causes that rendered the Wars of the Roses so prejudicial to the immediate development of the constitution.

8. Give some account of the municipal condition of Rome in the Middle Ages.

9. Write a character of one or two of the following persons: Anselm, Simon de Montfort, Edward III., the Emperor Frederick II., Philip the Fair, Maximilian I., Thomas Cromwell, the Earl of Clarendon, Maria Theresa, Danton, Kosciusko.

10. Can you distinguish between the real and the apparent disadvantages of centralisation in government?

CXIII.

1. The literary characteristics and importance of any of the following: Pindar, Herodotus, Plautus, Catullus.

2. The historical value of the Homeric poems.

3. 'The novel is to us what the drama was to Athens.' Discuss this.

4. Give an analysis of any two of the following characters in Shakespeare: Hamlet, Macbeth, Shylock, Falstaff, Beatrice.

5. What are the main differences between the poetry of the eighteenth and that of the nineteenth century?

6. What is meant by the following sayings?—'De mortuis nil nisi bonum.'—'The falsehood of extremes.'——'Might is right.'—'A little knowledge is a dangerous thing.'—'All men are equal.' How far are they true?

7. State briefly the arguments for and against restricting or prohibiting the sale of intoxicating drinks.

8. Describe, and comment on the results of, the following battles:—Lissa, Inkermann, Solferino, Sadowa, Sedan.

CXIV.

1. In what does the importance of Greek history consist?

2. What points of similarity do we find in the early history of Rome with that of any Greek state?

3. Describe the system of government in a Greek democracy. Would such a government correspond with the modern idea of a democracy?

4. What historical events are connected with any of the following: Corcyra, Cyprus, Lesbos, Samos, Sicily?

5. By what principal means were the Roman conquests in Italy secured?

6. Give some account of *one* of the following:—
    (*a*) The Laws of the Twelve Tables.
    (*b*) The conspiracy of Catilina.
    (*c*) The life of Constantine.

7. In what respects mainly was the change from republican to imperial government a gain to the Roman world?

8. Give the main points in *one* of the following:—
    (*a*) The Third Crusade.
    (*b*) The revolt of the United Provinces.
    (*c*) The career of Napoleon.

9. Give a short account of either: (1) The foreign relations of England in the reign of Elizabeth. *Or*, (2) The origin of the English power in India.

10. What is 'government by party'? Trace its origin in England.

11. Give some account of Burleigh, Falkland, Algernon Sidney, Bolingbroke, Somers, Peel.

CXV.

1. Paraphrase and explain :—

Neither is the Ancient Rule amisse, to bend Nature as a Wand, to a Contrary Extreme, whereby to set it right: Understanding it, when the Contrary Extreme is no Vice. Let not a man force a Habit upon himselfe, with a Perpetuall Continuance, but with some Intermission. For both the Pause, reinforceth the new Onset; And if a Man, that is not perfect, be ever in Practise, he shall as well practise his Errours, as his Abilities; And induce one Habite of both: And there is no Meanes to help this, but by Seasonable Intermissions. But let not a Man trust his Victorie over his Nature too farre; For Nature will lie buried a great Time, and yet revive, upon the Occasion or Temptation. Like as it with Æsopes Damosell, turned from a Catt to a Woman; who sate very demurely at the Boards End, til a Mouse ranne before her.

2. Discuss the influence of climate, food, soil, and the general aspect of Nature upon civilisation.

3. What is the value of historical dramas and novels to students of history.

4. What materials have we for a life of Shakespeare?

5. Compare the powers of expression possessed by painting and sculpture respectively.

6. Discuss the various methods of translating the Homeric poems.

7. What points is it most important to touch upon in drawing the character of a man?

CXVI.

1. Describe the formation of the confederacy of Delos, and its transition into the Athenian empire.

2. What degree of credibility can be accorded to the stories of the Roman kings?

3. What part did the Delphic oracle play in Greek history?

4. Illustrate the military and political genius of Philip of Macedon.

5. To what form of government would you refer the Roman constitution after the passing of the Hortensian law?

6. What circumstances favoured the Romans in their conquest of Italy?

7. Illustrate from Greek, Roman, or English history the tendency of authors to reverse the received estimate of historical characters.

8. Describe accurately, and indicate the effects of, *one* of the following battles: Marathon, Delium, Bannockburn, Malplaquet.

9. State and account for the local distribution of parties during the Great Rebellion.

10. What were the causes of the decline of monarchical power in England?

CXVII.

1. Explain clearly the following political terms:— 'empire,' 'nation,' 'state,' 'monarchy,' 'aristocracy,' 'oligarchy,' 'constitutional government.'

2. What were the chief points of strength or of weakness in the position of the Greeks during their contest with the Persians?

3. Illustrate from the events of the Peloponnesian war the difference in character of the Athenians and Lacedæmonians.

4. Contrast the empire of Rome with the empires of Athens and of Macedonia, and point out the importance of the differences between them.

5. What influence was exerted by the Crusades upon the social and political development of Western Europe?

6. Estimate the character and policy of Thomas Becket, and trace the course of his quarrel with Henry II.

7. How far can the Revolution of 1688 be regarded as marking an epoch in English constitutional history?

8. Whom do you consider the greatest English statesman of the eighteenth century? Give reasons for your answer.

9. Compare Gibbon, Macaulay, and Carlyle as writers of history.

10. Write a short biography of any *two* of the following: Demosthenes, Tiberius Gracchus, Hildebrand, Simon de Montfort, Cardinal Wolsey.

CXVIII.

1. Illustrate and explain the influence of Greece upon Rome in the two last centuries B.C.

2. Write short accounts of any four of the following: Cimon, Brasidas, Cato the Censor, Cinna, Mæcenas, Seneca, Polybius.

3. Describe the geographical position of Platæa, Miletus, Pylos, Brundisium, Saguntum, Agrigentum.

4. Give the dates and show the historical importance of—the burning of Sardis by the Athenians, the Peace of

Nicias, the battle of Pydna, the first consulship of Cæsar, the revolt of Civilis.

5. Contrast the powers of the House of Commons in the reigns of Edward III. and Elizabeth. What were the main causes of the change?

6. At what periods has the foreign policy of England been influenced by religious or commercial considerations?

7. Advantages and disadvantages of large as compared with small states?

8. Explain carefully the following terms: Myth, Comparative Method, Eclecticism, Autonomy.

9. Give a brief account of English prose literature during the eighteenth century. Had it any strongly marked characteristics?

10. The points of agreement and difference between Sophocles and Shakespeare. Illustrate by reference to particular plays.

11. Trace the successive steps in the development of any two of the following sciences: Botany, Geology, Astronomy, and Chemistry.

12. Describe briefly the characters and policy of Gregory VII., Richelieu, Edward IV., Frederick the Great.

13. 'Göthe said that the murder of Cæsar was the most senseless act that the Romans ever committed, and a truer word was never uttered.' Discuss this statement.

14. Sketch the characters of Cæsar and Cicero.

15. What do you know of Dante and Petrarch?

CXIX.

1. Describe the rise and fall of the early tyrannies in Greece.

2. Trace the establishment of the Roman rule over Italy, *or* over Spain, Gaul, and England.

3. What was the nature and value of the influence of the Papacy when at its height?

4. Estimate the importance in European history of the Edict of Nantes and its Revocation.

5. What changes in the boundaries of European states would be introduced by adopting the principle of Nationalities?

6. What do you know of any *three* of the following:—Themistocles, Demosthenes the Orator, Pyrrhus the Epirot, Q. Fabius Maximus Cunctator, Herod the Great, Agricola, Charlemagne, Hildebrand, Francis Bacon, Grotius, Burke?

7. Sketch briefly, fixing as many dates as you can, any *two* of the following:

   (*a*) The Wars between Greece and Persia.
   (*b*) The Crusades.
   (*c*) The fifteenth and sixteenth centuries as an age of discovery.
   (*d*) The Thirty Years' War.
   (*e*) The French Revolution and the First Empire.

CXX.

1. Trace the territorial increase of Prussia, since it became a kingdom. What are its claims, apart from the sword, to the first place in Germany?

2. 'It is the tendency of every nation to depreciate the share of its allies in any common achievement.' Illustrate from the military history of Rome and of England.

3. The most effective national boundaries under various conditions of civilisation.

4. Estimate the responsibility of the different religious parties in England on the score of religious persecution.

5. Virgil, Horace, and Lucan as patriotic poets.

6. The centres of Greek literary activity at different epochs.

7. Write characters of Alcibiades, Alexander, Augustus.

8. 'The Arthurian Epos of Tennyson is a vast anachronism.' Discuss this statement.

CXXI.

1. What influence did the geographical position of Sicily exercise upon ancient history?

2. The character of a Greek tyranny.

3. The causes and consequences of Greek colonisation.

4. What is known of the Etruscans?

5. In what directions can you trace the influence of religion in ancient Rome?

6. Why is the historical truth of the accounts of early Rome called into question?

7. Compare the amusements of the Greeks and the Romans.

8. Compare the position of women in Greece at different times and in different places.

9. Compare the predisposition to Federalism in Greece and Italy.

10. Illustrate from the history of Republican Rome the influence of roads and mountains.

11. What are the characteristic features of the freedom of Englishmen? On what basis do they rest?

12. Which event had the more important results,—the Battle of Crecy, or the Black Death?

13. Give the main steps in the abolition of Feudalism in England.

14. The chief features of the relations between England and Rome prior to the Reformation.

15. How was the progress of the Reformation in Germany and France arrested?

16. What do you consider the 'natural' boundaries of nations?

17. What are the reasons for the difficulty (1) of a speech in Thucydides, (2) of a chorus in Æschylus?

18. Draw out the main differences of idiom between Greek and Latin prose.

19. Cicero has been said to be first-rate only as a stylist, second-rate both as a politician and as an orator. Discuss this.

20. What amount of love for natural scenery is to be found in classical literature?

21. Criticise as subjects for artistic treatment *either* the Eclogues *or* the Georgics of Virgil, *or* the Essay on Man of Pope.

22. Show how the construction of the period in English prose has varied at different times. Has there been any corresponding difference in English poetry?

23. How far are the influences of foreign schools of poetry to be traced in Shakespeare *or* Milton?

24. What are the points of excellence in the composition of a sonnet, a song, a ballad, words for music?

25. The place of Tennyson among English poets.

26. How far are the unities of the drama observed in the Greek plays which you have read?

27. Compare the attitude of different religious revivals towards various forms of art.

SUBJECTS FOR ENGLISH ESSAYS.

I.

The influence of works of fiction.

1. Thackeray, English Humourists.
2. Carlyle, Essay on Scott.
3. Lord Lytton, Miscellaneous Prose Writings.
4. Lamb, Essay on Hogarth.

II.

What constitutes a great man?

1. Carlyle, Heroes and Hero-Worship.
2. Foster, Essays.
3. Landor, Imaginary Conversations.
4. Montaigne, Essays.

III.

'Give me the making of a nation's ballads, and I care not who makes their laws.'

1. Tyrtaeus.
2. The Jacobite Songs, and Lillibullero.
3. Béranger.
4. The Marseillaise.

IV.

The influence of climate upon national character.

1. Buckle, History of Civilisation.
2. H. N. Coleridge, Classic Poets.
3. Arnold, Lectures on Modern History.

V

The character and objects of a liberal education.

1. F. W. Farrar, Essays on a Liberal Education.
2. Montaigne, Essays.
3. Plato, Republic.

VI.

The good and evil done by the public press.

1. Milton, Areopagitica.
2. Johnson, Life of Milton.
3. Shelley, Defence of Poetry.
4. Kinglake, Invasion of the Crimea.
5. Macaulay, Essays and Speeches.

VII.

Court poets.

VIII.

The advantages and disadvantages of anonymous authorship.

IX.

'Homer was the greater genius, Virgil the better artist.'
Pope's Preface to the Iliad.

X.

Self-education.

XI.

How far do poetry, painting and sculpture differ from and resemble one another in their nature, capacity, and application?

XII.

Does the world grow happier or better?

XIII.

Originality.

XIV.

How far should the State attempt to guide opinion?

XV.

Heroism.

XVI.

The fitness of contemporary subjects for dramatic representation.

XVII.

The effects of the several professions on the character of those who pursue them.

XVIII.

Journalism.

XIX.

Fame is the spur that the clear spirit doth raise,
The last infirmity of noble minds.'

XX

'The tendency of institutions is to decay, of society to progress.' Discuss this statement.

XXI

A great nation's little wars.

XXII.

The causes of the decline and fall of the Roman empire.

XXIII.

The effects on patriotism of an increased familiarity with the life and character of other nations, and a due regard for their rights.

XXIV.

The social and moral effects of material civilisation.

XXV.

Penal legislation.

XXVI.

Multis utile bellum.

In what sense, and with what limitations, can it be said that war is beneficial?

XXVII

The limits of toleration.

XXVIII

Esprit de corps.

XXIX.

Truth is stranger than fiction.

XXX

The use of ridicule.

XXXI.

The claims of the ancient world on the attention and admiration of the modern.

XXXII.

The dangers of over-civilisation.

XXXIII.

Chivalry.

XXXIV.

The sources, growth, and probable future of existing class distinctions in England.

XXXV.

How far is the popularity of a literary work a true measure of its excellence?

XXXVI.

Courage.

XXXVII.

National character as an element in the success of colonies.

XXXVIII.

National character as shown in popular amusements.

XXXIX.

Loyalty.

The elements which constitute the sentiment of loyalty, and the various forms which it is capable of assuming.

XL.

The comparative advantages of school and private education.

XLI.

The connection of the literature of a nation with its character and political development.

XLII.

Are wars likely to diminish as nations become more civilised?

XLIII.

The influence of commercial prosperity upon national character.

XLIV.

The causes of the decay of nations.

XLV.

A letter to an Athenian of the time of Pericles describing those features in the political and social condition of England in the middle of the nineteenth century which would be likely to interest him most.

XLVI.

Discuss the alleged indifference of the best men to take part in public affairs.

XLVII.

The cause of the pleasure resulting from tragedy.

XLVIII.

The influence of veneration for the past, and desire for progress, on the character of societies and individuals.

XLIX.

'A froward retention of custom is as turbulent a thing as an innovation.'—*Bacon.*

L.

Is genius correctly defined as a 'transcendent capacity for taking trouble'?

LI.

Trial by Jury.

LII.

Autobiography.

LIII.

The advantages of an acquaintance with mathematical and physical science.

LIV.

Vote by Ballot.

LV.

On the use of History as a study.

LVI.

'When a Mammonite mother kills her babe for a burial
    fee,
And Timour-Mammon grins on a pile of children's
    bones,
Is it peace or war? better, war! loud war by land and
    by sea,
War with a thousand battles, and shaking a hundred
    thrones.'

LVII.

The relation of colonies to the parent state.

LVIII.

Nihilism, and how to deal with it.

LIX.

The influence of commerce upon politics.

LX.

Does the excellence of a work of fiction depend wholly or chiefly on its faithfulness to nature?

33 & 41 HIGH STREET, OXFORD,

AUGUST 1884.

JAMES THORNTON'S
List of Publications

CHIEFLY EDUCATIONAL,

MANY IN USE AT THE HIGHER SCHOOLS AND UNIVERSITIES.

CONTENTS.

	PAGE
CLASS BOOKS	8
CLASSICS AND TRANSLATIONS	10
LAW, HISTORY, AND POLITICAL PHILOSOPHY	4
MISCELLANEOUS	3
OXFORD STUDY GUIDES	6
PALÆSTRA OXONIENSIS	14
INDEX	16

Also sold by { SIMPKIN, MARSHALL, & CO. } London.
{ HAMILTON, ADAMS, & CO. }

A Catalogue of these Publications with fuller descriptions, some notices from the press and specimen pages, will be issued shortly, and will be forwarded gratis on application.

JAMES THORNTON *desires to direct attention to the accompanying List of* EDUCATIONAL WORKS, *many of which have now attained a wide circulation.*

The Authors and Compilers are mostly scholars of repute, as well as of large experience in teaching.

Any notices of errors or defects in these publications will be gratefully received and acknowledged.

The Books can generally be procured through local Booksellers in town and country; but if at any time difficulty should arise, JAMES THORNTON *will feel obliged by direct communication on the subject.*

MISCELLANEOUS.

THE LATIN PRAYER BOOK OF CHARLES II.; or, an Account of the Liturgia of Dean Durel, together with a Reprint and Translation of the Catechism therein contained, with Collations, Annotations, and Appendices by the Rev. CHARLES MARSHALL, M.A., Chaplain to the Lord Mayor of London, 1849-1850; and WILLIAM W. MARSHALL, B.A., of the Inner Temple, late Scholar of Hertford College, Oxford. Demy 8vo. cloth, 10s. 6d. [*Recently published.*

'Is a distinct and important contribution to the Evangelical side of the Sacramentarian controversy.'—BRITISH QUARTERLY REVIEW.

'We have great pleasure in commending this work as a learned and valuable contribution to our liturgical literature.'—RECORD, *November* 3, 1882.

CANONS OF THE SECOND COUNCIL OF ORANGE A.D. 529. With an Introduction, Translation, and Notes. By the Rev. F. H. WOODS, B.D., Fellow of St. John's College, Oxford. Crown 8vo. 2s.

RECORD of the UNIVERSITY BOAT RACE, 1829-1880, and of the COMMEMORATION DINNER, 1881. Compiled by GEO. G. T. TREHERNE, O.U.B.C., and J. H. D. GOLDIE, C.U.B.C. With Illustrations, 4to. cloth, 10s. 6d.; or, printed on large handmade paper, with China paper impressions of the Plates, price 30s. (only 250 copies printed, each numbered and initialled).

NEW AND REVISED EDITION, bringing the work up to 1884. 8vo. cloth, 6s.

An UNDERGRADUATE'S TRIP to ITALY and ATTICA in the WINTER of 1880-1. By J. L. THOMAS, Balliol College Oxford. Crown 8vo. 5s.

THE LIVES AND EPISTLES OF GIFFORD AND BUNYAN. By the Rev. T. A. BLYTH, B.A., Queen's College, Oxford.
[*In the press.*

The RECENT DEPRESSION of TRADE, its Nature, its Causes, and the Remedies which have been suggested for it; being the Oxford Cobden Prize Essay for 1879. By WALTER E. SMITH, B.A., New College. Crown 8vo. cloth, 3s. 6d.

LAW, HISTORY, & POLITICAL PHILOSOPHY.

THOMAS HOBBES, of MALMESBURY, LEVIATHAN; or, the Matter, Forme, and Power of a Commonwealth. A New Reprint. With a facsimile of the original fine engraved Title. Medium 8vo. cloth, 12s. 6d.

A small edition of 250 copies only, on Dutch hand-made paper, medium 8vo. 18s.

Students' Edition, crown 8vo. cloth 8s. 6d. [*Just published.*

'In matters of reprints, such as this is, it is always well to retain as much as possible the old spelling, and the old form of printing. By this means we are constantly reminded that we are reading a seventeenth century writer, and not a nineteenth; and hence students will apply more checks to their process of reasoning than they might be inclined to do if the book were printed in modern form. This is, we are glad to say, applicable to the present excellent reprint, which is issued in old spelling, and contains in the margin the figures of the pagination of the first edition.'
THE ANTIQUARY, *October* 1881.

'We have received from Mr. James Thornton, of Oxford, an excellent reprint of Hobbes's "Leviathan." The book is one which is not always easy to obtain; and a satisfactory reprint at a reasonable price may do more to advance the knowledge of Hobbes's philosophy than one of the condensed handbooks which are now extensively popular.'
WESTMINSTER REVIEW, *January* 1882.

THE ELEMENTS OF LAW, NATURAL AND POLITIC. By THOMAS HOBBES, of Malmesbury. The first complete and correct Edition, with a Preface and Critical Notes. By FERDINAND JOENNIES, Ph.D. To which are subjoined selected pieces of unprinted MSS. of THOMAS HOBBES. [*In the press; ready in October.*

BEHEMOTH; or, The LONG PARLIAMENT. By THOMAS HOBBES, of Malmesbury. For the first time Edited after the Original MS., with many Additions and Corrections. By FERDINAND JOENNIES, Ph.D. [*In the press.*

REMARKS on the USE and ABUSE of SOME POLITICAL TERMS. By the late Right Hon. Sir GEORGE CORNEWALL LEWIS, Bart., sometime Student of Christ Church, Oxford. A New Edition, with Notes and Appendix. By Sir ROLAND KNYVET WILSON, Bart., M.A., Barrister-at-Law; Reader in Indian Law, and late Fellow of King's College, Cambridge; Author of 'History of Modern English Law.' Crown 8vo. 6s.

An ESSAY on the GOVERNMENT of DEPENDENCIES. By the late Right Hon. Sir GEORGE CORNEWALL LEWIS, Bart., sometime Student of Christ Church, Oxford. A New Reprint. [*In the press.*

QUESTIONS and EXERCISES in POLITICAL ECONOMY, with References to Adam Smith, Ricardo, John Stuart Mill, Fawcett, Thorold Rogers, Bonamy Price, Twiss, Senior, Macleod, and others. Adapted to the Oxford Pass and Honour and the Cambridge Ordinary B.A. Examinations. Arranged and edited by W. P. EMERTON, M.A., D.C.L., Christ Church, Oxford. Crown 8vo. cloth, 3s. 6d.

MONTENEGRO: being the Stanhope Prize Essay for 1884. By WILLIAM CARR, Commoner of University College, Oxford. 8vo. paper covers (106 pages), 2s. 6d. [*Just published.*

LAW, HISTORY, AND POLITICAL PHILOSOPHY—
continued.

DE CONJECTURIS ULTIMARUM VOLUNTATUM. Dissertatio pro Gradu Doctoris in Jure Civili. By WOLSELEY P. EMERTON, D.C.L., Christ Church. 8vo. sewed (110 pages, 2s. 6d. [*Just published.*

An ABRIDGMENT of ADAM SMITH'S INQUIRY into the NATURE and CAUSES of the WEALTH of NATIONS. By W. P. EMERTON, M.A., D.C.L. Crown 8vo. cloth, 6s.

This work (based on Jeremiah Joyce's Abridgment) originally appeared in two parts and is now republished after careful revision, with Additional Notes, Appendices, and a Complete Index.

The above can be had in two Parts. Part I. Books I. and II. 3s. 6d. Part II. Books III., IV. and V. 3s. 6d.

OUTLINES of JURISPRUDENCE. For the Use of Students. By B. R. WISE, B.A., late Scholar of Queen's College, Oxford; Oxford Cobden Prizeman, 1878. Crown 8vo. cloth, 5s.

This book is intended to be a critical and explanatory commentary upon the Jurisprudence text-books in common use; and it endeavours to present a precise and coherent view of all the topics upon which these touch.

'The student of jurisprudence will certainly find the work suggestive and helpful.'
THE ATHENÆUM, *July* 15, 1882.

OUTLINES of ENGLISH CONSTITUTIONAL HISTORY. By BRITIFFE CONSTABLE SKOTTOWE, M.A., late Scholar of New College, Oxford. Crown 8vo. cloth, 3s. 6d.

The object of this book is to assist beginners in reading Constitutional History by arranging in order outlines of the growth of the most important Institutions.

An ANALYSIS of the ENGLISH LAW of REAL PROPERTY, chiefly from Blackstone's Commentary, with Tables and Indexes. By GORDON CAMPBELL, M.A., Author of 'An Analysis of Austin's Lectures on Jurisprudence,' and of 'A Compendium of Roman Law.' Crown 8vo. cloth, 3s. 6d.

An ANALYSIS of JUSTINIAN'S INSTITUTES of ROMAN LAW, with Tables. [*In preparation.*

A CHRONOLOGICAL SUMMARY of the CHIEF REAL PROPERTY STATUTES, with their more important Provisions. For the Use of Law Students. By P. F. ALDRED, M.A., D.C.L. Crown 8vo. 2s.

ELEMENTARY QUESTIONS on the LAW of PROPERTY, REAL and PERSONAL. Supplemented by Advanced Questions on the Law of Contracts. With Copious References throughout, and an Index of Legal Terms. Crown 8vo. cloth, 3s. 6d.

The SPECIAL STATUTES required by Candidates for the School of Jurisprudence at Oxford. Fcp. 8vo. sewed, 2s. 6d. With brief Notes and Translations by a B.C.L. Cloth, 5s.

OXFORD STUDY GUIDES.

A SERIES OF HANDBOOKS TO EXAMINATIONS.

Edited by F. S. PULLING, M.A., Exeter College.

THE object of this Series is to guide Students in their reading for the different examinations. The amount of time wasted at present, simply through ignorance of the way to read, is so great that the Editor and Authors feel convinced of the necessity for some such handbooks, and they trust that these Guides will at least do something to prevent in the future the misapplication of so much industry.

Each volume will be confined to one branch of study, and will include an account of the various Scholarships and Prizes offered by the University or the Colleges in its department; and will be undertaken by a writer whose experience qualifies him to speak with authority on the subject.

The books will contain extracts from the University Statutes relating to the Examinations, with an attempt to explain them as they exist, and advice as to what to read and how to read; how to prepare subjects for examination, and how to answer papers; a few specimen questions, extracts from the Regulations of the Board of Studies, and a list of books.

THEOLOGY. By the Rev. F. H. WOODS, B.D., Fellow of St. John's College. Crown 8vo. cloth, 2s. 6d.

ENTRANCE CLASSICAL SCHOLARSHIPS. By S. H. JEYES, M.A., Lecturer in Classics at University College. Crown 8vo. cloth, 2s. 6d.

'It is quite refreshing to find a guide to an examination that so thoroughly discourages cram.'—SCHOOL GUARDIAN, *June* 20, 1881.

'This is a smart book, and a useful comment on the present method of awarding scholarships. There is a certain frank cynicism in much of the advice, as when Mr. JEYES remarks, "It is no good wearing out your trousers in a study chair, if you do not set your brains to work;" or that it "is quite useless to play at hide-and seek with examiners who are familiar with every turn and twist in the game;" and there seems little doubt that a clever boy, coached by him on his method, would get a scholarship.'—SPECTATOR, *Aug.* 27, 1881.

'Mr. Jeyes has provided parents and teachers with an excellent manual by which to guide their sons or pupils in preparing for University Scholarships...... He gives directions as to the best way of preparing for the different sorts of papers ..... and also for the best way of tackling with the paper when confronted with it in actual examination. The observations are of the most practical kind...... The book is well done, and ought to be useful.'—THE ACADEMY, *June* 18, 1881.

JAMES THORNTON, 33 & 41 HIGH STREET, OXFORD.

OXFORD STUDY GUIDES—*continued.*

HONOUR CLASSICAL MODERATIONS. By L. R. FARNELL, M.A., Fellow of Exeter College. Crown 8vo. cloth, 2*s.* 6*d.*

'It is full of useful and scholarly suggestions which many hard-reading men will be thankful for....... With hints as to the line of reading to be adopted, and the books to be taken up so as to make the most of their time and to read to the best advantage.'
SCHOOL GUARDIAN, *November* 4, 1881.

LITERÆ HUMANIORES. By E. B. IWAN-MÜLLER, M.A., New College.
[*Shortly.*

MODERN HISTORY. By F. S. PULLING, M.A., Exeter College. *Will be published as soon as possible after the new scheme is finally sanctioned.*

NATURAL SCIENCE. By E. B. POULTON, M.A., Keble College.

JURISPRUDENCE and CIVIL LAW. By W. P. EMERTON, M.A., D.C.L., Christ Church. [*In preparation.*

ARITHMETIC.

Just published.

ARITHMETIC for SCHOOLS. Based on principles of Cause and Effect. By the Rev. FREDERICK SPARKS, M.A., Mathematical Master, the High School, Plymouth, and late Lecturer of Worcester College, Oxford. Crown 8vo. cloth (416 pages), 4*s.* 6*d.*

It may perhaps appear somewhat rash to add another to the many text books on Arithmetic already in use. It is believed, however, that the present work will be found to contain some features sufficiently distinctive and valuable to warrant its appearance.

The chief aim of the work is to place prominently before the student the fact that the principle of 'cause and effect' is as applicable to Arithmetic as to other sciences, and that by working on this plan he may obtain his results in about half the time required by other methods. In each division of the subject this is shown by a typical example worked out in full, followed by ample exercises, with examination papers at regular intervals. The more complex parts of fractions and decimals are introduced later, so that the pupil may reach as early as possible the more interesting part of his work, the arithmetic of ordinary life. The so called 'inverse rules' are learnt at the same time as the 'direct rules,' and thus the difficulties of proportion wholly disappear. A careful selection of questions set by the Universities, Civil Service, and Army Examination Boards, and other educational bodies, has been placed at the end of the volume.

The ANSWERS to the above are published in a separate form.

CLASS BOOKS.

MELETEMATA; or, SELECT LATIN PASSAGES IN PROSE AND VERSE FOR UNPREPARED TRANSLATION. Arranged by the Rev. P. J. F. GANTILLON, M.A., sometime Scholar of St. John's College, Cambridge, Classical Master in Cheltenham College. Crown 8vo. cloth, 4s. 6d.

The object of this volume is to furnish a collection of about 250 passages, graduated in difficulty, and adapted to the various Examinations in which 'Unprepared Translation' finds a place.

'The work is nicely got up, and is altogether the best of the kind with which we are acquainted.'—THE SCHOOLMASTER, *December* 3, 1881.

'We find this collection to be very judiciously made, and think it one of the best which has yet been published.'—EDUCATIONAL TIMES, *April* 1, 1881.

Forming a Companion Volume to the above.

MELETEMATA GRÆCA; being a Selection of Passages, Prose and Verse, for unprepared Translation. By the Rev. P. J. F. GANTILLON, M.A. [*In the press.*

SELECTED PIECES for TRANSLATION into LATIN PROSE. Selected and arranged by the Rev. H. C. OGLE, M.A. Head Master of Magdalen College School, and T. CLAYTON, M.A. Crown 8vo. cloth, 4s. 6d.

This selection is intended for the use of the highest forms in Schools and for University Students for Honour Examinations, for whom it was felt that a small and compact book would be most serviceable.

'The selection has been made with much care and the passages which we have more particularly examined are very appropriate for translation.'
SCHOOL GUARDIAN, *June* 7, 1879.

LATIN and GREEK VERSIONS of some of the SELECTED PIECES for TRANSLATION. Collected and arranged by the Rev. H. C. OGLE, M.A., Head Master of Magdalen College School; and THOMAS CLAYTON, M.A., Trinity College, Oxford. Crown 8vo. 5s. [*Just ready.*

This Key is for the use of Tutors only, and is issued on the understanding that it does not get into the hands of any pupil.

For the convenience of Schoolmasters and Tutors these Versions are also issued in another form viz. on separate leaves ready for distribution to pupils, thereby saving the necessity of dictating or copying. They are done up in packets of twenty-five each, and not less than twenty-five sets (= 76 packets) can be supplied at a time. Price—Thirty-five Shillings net.

DAMON; or, The ART of GREEK IAMBIC MAKING. By the Rev. J. HERBERT WILLIAMS, M.A., Composition Master in S. Nicholas College, Lancing; late Demy of Magdalen College. Fcp. 8vo. 1s. 6d.

This small treatise claims as its merit that it really teaches Greek Iambic writing on a system, and this system is based on no arbitrary analysis of the Iambic line, but on the way in which the scholar practically regards it in making verses himself.

A Key, for Tutors only. Fcp. 8vo. cloth, 3s. 6d.

CLASS BOOKS—*continued.*

SHORT TABLES and NOTES on GREEK and LATIN GRAMMAR. By W. E. W. COLLINS, M.A., Jesus College. Second Edition, revised. Crown 8vo. cloth, 2s.

ARS SCRIBENDI LATINE; or, Aids to Latin Prose Composition. In the form of an Analysis of Latin Idioms. By B. A. EDWARDS, B.A., late Scholar of Jesus College, Oxford. Crown 8vo. 1s.

ARITHMETIC FOR SCHOOLS. Based on principles of Cause and Effect. By the Rev. FREDERICK SPARKS, M.A., Mathematical Master, the High School, Plymouth, and late Lecturer of Worcester College, Oxford. Crown 8vo. cloth (416 pages), 4s. 6d. [*Just ready.*

ALGEBRAICAL QUESTIONS AND EXERCISES. For the Use of Candidates for Matriculation, Responsions, and First Public Examinations, and the Oxford and Cambridge Local and Certificate Examinations. Crown 8vo. 2s.

ARITHMETICAL QUESTIONS AND EXERCISES. For the Use of Candidates for Matriculation, Responsions, and First Public Examinations, and the Oxford and Cambridge Local and Certificate Examinations. Crown 8vo. 1s. 6d.

QUESTIONS AND EXERCISES IN ADVANCED LOGIC. For the Use of Candidates for the Honour Moderation Schools. Crown 8vo. 1s. 6d.

The RUDIMENTS OF LOGIC, with Tables and Examples. By F. E. WEATHERLY, M.A. Fcp. 8vo. cloth limp, 1s 6d.

'Here is everything needful for a beginner.'—EDUCATIONAL TIMES.
'Is a clever condensation of first principles.'—SCHOOL GUARDIAN.

QUESTIONS in LOGIC, Progressive and General. By FREDERIC E. Weatherley, M.A., late Scholar of Brasenose College, Oxford. Fcp. 8vo. paper covers, 1s. [*Just published.*

A FEW NOTES on the GOSPELS. By W. E. W. COLLINS, M.A., Jesus College. New Edition. Crown 8vo. paper covers, 1s. 6d.

ARITHMETICAL AIDS to RESPONSIONS; containing Concise Rules and Examples worked out. Crown 8vo. paper cover, 1s. [*Just published.*

CLASSICS AND TRANSLATIONS.

The NICOMACHEAN ETHICS of ARISTOTLE. Books I.–IV. and Book X. Chap. 6 to 9, being the portion required in the Oxford Pass School, with Notes, &c. for the use of Passmen. By E. L. HAWKINS, M.A., late Postmaster of Merton College. Demy 8vo. cloth, 8s. 6d. Interleaved with writing paper, 10s. 6d.

The NICOMACHEAN ETHICS of ARISTOTLE. A New Translation, with an Introduction, a Marginal Analysis, and Explanatory Notes. By Rev. D. P. CHASE, D.D., Fellow of Oriel College, and Principal of St. Mary Hall, Oxford. Fourth Edition, revised. Crown 8vo. cloth, 4s. 6d.

The ELEMENTS of ARISTOTLE'S LOGIC, following the order of Trendelenburg, with Introduction, English translation, and Notes. By THOMAS CASE, M.A., Tutor of Corpus Christi College, and sometime Fellow of Brasenose College. [*Preparing.*

ARISTOTLE'S ORGANON: Translations from the Organon of Aristotle, comprising those Sections of Mr. Magrath's Selections required for Honour Moderations. By W. SMITH, B.A. New College, and ALAN G. SUMNER GIBSON, M.A., late Scholar of Corpus Christi College Oxford. Crown 8vo. 2s. 6d.

The POETICS of ARISTOTLE. The text after Vahlen, with an Introduction, a New Translation, Explanatory and Critical Notes, and an Appendix on the Greek Drama. [*In preparation.*

DEMOSTHENES on the CROWN. The Text after BAITER. With an Introduction, a New Translation, Notes and Indices. By FRANCIS P. SIMPSON, B.A., Balliol College, Craven Scholar, 1877. Demy 8vo. cloth, 10s. 6d.

* FROM THE PREFACE.—Several of the Notes—which I have tried to make as concise as possible—may appear unnecessary to a scholar; but they have been inserted for the practical reason that the obstacles they should remove have been felt by some of the many pupils with whom I have read this speech.

The main difficulty which Demosthenes presents to the student lies in the close logical connection of his arguments; and most commentaries consist largely of translation or paraphase. Paraphase is dangerous, as it may lead a novice to a belief that he quite understands a piece of Latin or Greek, when he is some way from doing so. I have, therefore, taken the bull by the horns, and have given a continuous rendering, as close as I could decently make it. Its aim is purely commentatorial—to save its weight in notes. It is intended to show what Demosthenes said, but not how well he said it. And, I may say, I believe that every lecturer and tutor in Oxford will admit that an undergraduate, or sixth-form boy, cannot get full value out of reading the De Corona without such help.

In Introduction I. will be found a sketch of Athenian history, as far as is necessary for the thorough understanding of this Oration. In Introduction II. a precis of the oration of Aeschines, as well as that of Demosthenes, is prefixed to a brief analysis of the two speeches considered as an attack and a defence.

CLASSICS AND TRANSLATIONS—*continued.*

EXTRACTS FROM LETTERS AND REVIEWS.

'Accept my best thanks for your presentation copy of Mr. Simpson's edition of the ORATION FOR THE CROWN, which I have no doubt will be gratefully accepted by professional scholars and the educated laity.'—Prof. BLACKIE.

'It seems to me very well done and likely to be of great use. I notice with pleasure that several mistakes of other translations and editions are tacitly corrected. Possibly there might be a little more freedom in the translation without merely paraphrasing; but this is no doubt very difficult to do except at the cost of extra notes, and I believe you are quite right in economising notes, which tend now to overlay and efface the texts of the classics.'—S. H. BUTCHER, Esq., Fellow of University College, Oxford, and Professor of Greek in the University of Edinburgh.

'I have made use of it for the last two of a course of lectures on the speech with profit to myself, and I think it is likely to be appreciated.'
Rev. T. L. PAPILLON, Fellow of New College, Oxford.

'It seems to me likely to be very useful.'
A. SIDGWICK, Esq., Fellow of Corpus Christi College, Oxford.

'I am struck with the scholarly tone of all that I have seen. Some of the notes seem models of good scholarship and exegesis.'
A. T. BARTON, Esq., Fellow of Pembroke College, Oxford.

'Its closeness and accuracy will make it very useful for many students.'
Rev. W. W. MERRY, Lincoln College, Oxford.

'One or two test passages that I have already looked at show that delicate points have been considered and common traps avoided. The abstract of the speech of Aeschines is an especially useful feature, and so is the copious index.'
Rev. J. R. KING, Fellow and Tutor, Oriel College, Oxford.

'I have read Mr. Simpson's "De Corona" with great interest. The translation and the notes seem to be alike admirable, and to furnish the student with everything necessary for gaining a scholarly knowledge of this masterpiece of Greek oratory.'
Rev. G. H. HESLOP, M.A., late Head Master of St. Bees' School, and formerly Fellow of Queen's College, Oxford.

'Mr. Simpson's . . . text is probably the best yet published in England; while the index of words and phrases should prove a valuable help to students and editors. . . . The volume is very well got up.'—ATHENÆUM, *December 2, 1882.*

'This is a handsome edition of the text, with translation opposite, and notes at the foot of the page. Of the translation, Mr. Simpson says that " it is intended to show" what Demosthenes said, not how well he said it." Its aim is "purely commentatorial,' and we believe that this aim is fully attained. It differs alike from loose paraphrase on the one hand, and on the other from those baldly literal versions which, by the seductive promise of close fidelity to the text, beguile the unhappy passman to his destruction, and make impossible a task which was at first only difficult. The general reader is supplied with a speech which can be read, and might conceivably be spoken; while the young student may get most valuable hints by observing closely how the structure of the original is dealt with. The notes, mainly grammatical, contain little that is striking, but give in short compass much help towards the appreciation of Greek idiom.'—SPECTATOR, *October 7, 1882.*

'. . . It is an excellent specimen of manly, straightforward English, and as far removed as possible from the atrocious slipslop which translators—by a law, as it would seem to be, of their being—most commonly affect. This edition, however, deserves unstinted praise, not merely for what it gives the student, but also for what it refrains from giving him. The notes are concise, and for the most part grammatical; but whatever they are they are always practical, and have been inserted for the practical reason that the obstacles they should remove have been felt by some of the many pupils with whom Mr. Simpson has read this speech. . . . Meanwhile it is our pleasant duty to congratulate Mr. Simpson on the entire success with which he has executed his task. Coming after so many deplorable examples of "how not to do it" in the matter of translations from the classics, this brilliant example of "how to do it" is doubly welcome.'
ST. JAMES'S GAZETTE, *November 11, 1882.*

CLASSICS AND TRANSLATIONS—*continued*.

The PHILIPPIC ORATIONS of CICERO. A New Translation. By the Rev. JOHN RICHARD KING, M.A., Fellow and Tutor of Oriel College, Oxford. Crown 8vo. cloth, 4s. 6d.

'The translation is forcible and fluent, and, so far as we have compared it with the original, accurate.'—ATHENÆUM, *Dec.* 7, 1878.

'The translation is evidently the work of a competent scholar......who is beyond all question master of the text.'—SPECTATOR, *July* 12, 1879.

The FIRST and SECOND PHILIPPIC ORATIONS of CICERO. A New Translation. By the Rev. J. R. KING, M.A. Fourth Edition. Crown 8vo. 1s. 6d.

The FIRST FOUR PHILIPPIC ORATIONS of CICERO. A New Translation. By the Rev. J. R. KING, M.A. Crown 8vo. 2s. 6d.

The SPEECH of CICERO for CLUENTIUS. Translated into English, with an Introduction and Notes. By W. PETERSON, M.A., late Scholar of Corpus Christi College, Oxford; Principal and Professor of Classics, University College, Dundee; late Assistant to the Professor of Humanity in the University of Edinburgh. Crown 8vo. cloth, 3s. 6d.

'We have gone over the translation with some care, and we have found it of uniform excellence. If any young scholar ever takes Niebuhr's advice about translating the speech, he could not do better than compare his own with this version before he began to retranslate it. The translation is not only accurate, but it abounds in neat and scholarly renderings of awkward Latin idioms.'—GLASGOW HERALD, *September* 1, 1882.

'This is a sound and scholarly piece of work......The version is faithful without being unduly literal......both the Introduction and the Translation will prove trustworthy guides to the young student......For the more advanced scholar the chief interest of the book lies in the valuable notes with which Prof. Nettleship has enriched it. These deal both with the diction and with the text, and are as suggestive as might be expected from the reputation of the Oxford Professor of Latin.'
The ACADEMY, *Jan.* 27, 1883.

The LETTERS of CICERO after the DEATH of CÆSAR: being Part V. of Mr. Watson's Selection. A New Translation by S. H. JEYES, M.A., Lecturer in Classics at University College, Oxford. Crown 8vo. cloth, 2s. 6d. [*Just published.*]

'There is much to praise in the translation; nearly every letter contains some striking and suggestive expressions which will be useful to students......Mr. Jeyes often shows great skill in the management of words.'—OXFORD MAGAZINE, *June* 6, 1883.

'The work is intended for the use of candidates for Classical Honours in Moderations, and supposing them to need a translation at all, they could scarcely have a better one. Besides help in reading their Cicero, students may gain an insight into differences between English and Latin idioms, which will be most useful to them in writing Latin Prose ... happy turns of this kind are to be met with in every letter. ... We might read page after page without discovering that the work was a translation, yet a comparison of these very pages with the original would probably fail to reveal the least inaccuracy.'—JOURNAL OF EDUCATION, *Oct.* 1, 1883.

The AGAMEMNON of ÆSCHYLUS. A new Prose Translation. Crown 8vo. cloth limp, 2s.

CLASSICS AND TRANSLATIONS—*continued*.

The HECUBA of EURIPIDES. Newly translated into English Prose by A. S. WALPOLE, M.A., late Scholar of Worcester College, Oxford; Joint Editor of the Greek Text. *[In the press.*

LIVY'S HISTORY of ROME. The Fifth, Sixth, and Seventh Books. A Literal Translation from the Text of MADVIG, with Historical Introductions, Summary to each Book, and Explanatory Notes. By a First Classman. Crown 8vo. 4s. 6d.

THE SATIRES OF JUVENAL. A new English Translation, with an Introduction and Marginal Analysis and Notes. By S. H. JEYES, M.A., late Lecturer in Classics at University College, Oxford. Crown 8vo. cloth, 3s. 6d. *[Just ready.*

A SYNOPSIS of LIVY'S HISTORY of the SECOND PUNIC WAR. Books XXI.–XXIV. With Appendices, Notes, Maps, and Plans. By J. B. WORCESTER, M.A. Second Edition. Fcp. 8vo. cloth, 2s. 6d.

The MENO of PLATO. A New Translation, with Introduction and Explanatory Notes, for the use of Students. Crown 8vo. cloth limp 1s. 6d.

A SYNOPSIS and SUMMARY of the REPUBLIC of PLATO. With a Prefatory Excursus upon the Platonic Philosophy, and Short Notes. By GEORGE WILLIAM GENT, M.A., Tutor of Keble College, Oxford. *[Preparing.*

PLUTARCH'S LIVES of the GRACCHI. Translated from the Text of Sintenis, with Introduction, Marginal Analysis, and Appendices. By W. W. MARSHALL, B.A., late Scholar of Hertford College. Crown 8vo. paper covers, 1s. 6d., or cloth, 2s.

A SYNOPSIS and SUMMARY of the ANNALS of TACITUS. Books I.—VI. With Introduction, Notes, and Indexes. By G. W. GENT, M.A., Tutor of Keble College, Oxford. Crown 8vo. cloth, 3s. 6d.

A FEW NOTES on the ANNALS of TACITUS. Books I to IV. For Passmen. Crown 8vo. *[In the press.*

The ÆNEID of VIRGIL. Books I. to VI. Translated into English Prose. By T. CLAYTON, M.A. Crown 8vo. cloth, 2s.

The ÆNEID of VIRGIL. A new Prose Translation. By THOMAS CLAYTON, M.A., Trinity College, Oxford. *[In preparation.*

PALÆSTRA OXONIENSIS.

The object of this Series is to furnish Exercises and Test Papers for Candidates preparing for the various Examinations at our Public Schools and Universities.

QUESTIONS and EXERCISES for MATRICULATION and RESPONSIONS. CONTENTS: (1) Grammatical Questions in Greek and Latin; (2) Materials for Latin Prose; (3) Questions on Authors. Sixth Edition. Crown 8vo. cloth, 3s. 6d.

CRITICA CLASSICA, Part. I.; being Answers to the Grammatical Portion of the 'Questions and Exercises for Matriculation and Responsions.' By W. W. CROUCH, M.A., and A. T. CROUCH, B.A. Crown 8vo. cloth. [*Just published.*

This work has been undertaken at the request of many correspondents who have expressed the opinion that it would form a valuable supplement to the 'Questions and Exercises,' and would be helpful to teachers and students alike. Great care has been taken to ensure precise accuracy of scholarship, and each question has been fully answered in the hope that the student may find it a complete and trustworthy test of his grammatical knowledge.

QUESTIONS and EXERCISES for CLASSICAL SCHOLARSHIPS. CONTENTS: (1) Critical Grammar Questions in Greek and Latin; (2) Unseen passages for translation. Adapted to the Oxford and Cambridge Schools Certificate and the Oxford First Public Examinations. Second Edition, corrected and enlarged. Crown 8vo. cloth, 3s. 6d.

CRITICA CLASSICA, Part II.; being Elucidations of the Critical Portion of 'Questions and Exercises for Classical Scholarships.' [*In preparation.*

FROM THE PREFACE.—The utility of a book like the present, provided it be properly done, will hardly be doubted by practical teachers.... Examination is not only a test, but a means of knowledge. It is the rough road by which we find out how much we do not know. Still more, nothing better strengthens our grasp of familiar facts than handling them in many ways and grouping them in different combinations. Nor does it wholly 'come by nature' to be able to discern the exact bearing of a question. Answers given at the examination table, as at the witness box, oftener say too much than too little. The golden rule is to answer the question—the whole question if possible; at any rate nothing but the question. But practice alone can give this faculty, while its importance in bestowing symmetry, neatness, and precision of style need hardly be named.

QUESTIONS and EXERCISES for CLASSICAL SCHOLARSHIPS. Second Division. CONTENTS: (1) Historical and General Questions; (2) Subjects for English Essays. Crown 8vo. cloth, 3s. 6d.

PALÆSTRA OXONIENSIS—*continued*.

QUESTIONS and EXERCISES in ELEMENTARY MATHEMATICS. CONTENTS: (1) Arithmetic; (2) Algebra; (3) Euclid. Third Edition, enlarged. Adapted to Matriculation, Responsions, and First Public Examinations, and the Oxford and Cambridge Local and Certificate Examinations. Crown 8vo, cloth, 3s. 6d. With ANSWERS, 5s. The ANSWERS separately, paper covers, 1s. 6d.

QUESTIONS and EXERCISES in ELEMENTARY LOGIC, DEDUCTIVE and INDUCTIVE; with Index of Logical Terms. Crown 8vo. cloth. (New Edition in the press.)

QUESTIONS and EXERCISES in RUDIMENTARY DIVINITY. CONTENTS: (1) Old Testament; (2) New Testament; (3) The Thirty-Nine Articles; (4) Greek Passages for Translation. Adapted to the Oxford Pass and the Oxford and Cambridge Certificate Examinations. Second Edition. Crown 8vo. cloth, 3s. 6d.

ELEMENTARY QUESTIONS on the LAW of PROPERTY, REAL and PERSONAL. Supplemented by Advanced Questions on the Law of Contracts. With Copious References throughout, and an Index of Legal Terms. Crown 8vo. cloth, 3s. 6d.

QUESTIONS and EXERCISES in POLITICAL ECONOMY, with References to Adam Smith, Ricardo, John Stuart Mill, Fawcett, J. E. Thorold Rogers, Bonamy Price, Twiss, Senior, and others. Crown 8vo. cloth, 3s. 6d.

This volume consists of Questions mainly taken from various Examination Papers with references in the case of the easier questions, and hints, and in some cases formal statements of the arguments *pro* and *con*. to the more difficult questions. There are also two Appendixes on the debated questions—'Is Political Economy a Science?' and 'Is Political Economy Selfish?'

QUESTIONS and EXERCISES in ENGLISH HISTORY, with References to the best authorities. Arranged and Edited by F. S. PULLING, M.A., Exeter College. Adapted to the Oxford Pass and Honour Schools, and the Cambridge History Tripos and Ordinary B.A. Examinations. [*In preparation.*

JAMES THORNTON, 33 & 41 HIGH STREET, OXFORD.

INDEX.

	PAGE
Æschylus—Agamemnon, Translation of	12
Aldred (D.C.L.) P. F.—Questions on Real Property	5
— Chief Real Property Statutes	5
Arithmetical Aids to Responsions	9
Blyth, Rev. T. A.—Lives and Letters of Gifford and Bunyan	3
Campbell, Gordon.—Analysis of Real Property Law	5
Carr, William. — Montenegro (Stanhope Essay)	4
Case (M.A.) Thomas.—Aristotle's Logic	10
Chase (D.D.) Rev. D. P.—Aristotle's Ethics	10
Clayton, Thomas.—Selected Pieces for Translation	8
— Virgil's Æneid	13
Collins (M.A.) W. E. W.—Greek and Latin Grammar Notes	9
— Notes on the Gospels	9
— Rudimentary Divinity	15
Crouch (M.A.) W. W.—Critica Classica, Part I.	14
Crouch (B.A.) A. T.—Critica Classica, Part I.	14
Edwards, Rev. B. A.—Ars Scribendi Latine	9
Emerton (D.C.L.) W. P.—Questions in Political Economy	4
— De Conjecturis &c.	5
— Abridgment of Adam Smith	5
— Jurisprudence and Civil Law	7
Furnell (M.A.) L. R.—Classical Moderation	7
Gantillon (M.A.) Rev. P. J. F.—Meletemata	8
— Meletemata Græca	8
Gent (M.A.) Rev. G. W.—Republic of Plato	13
— Annales of Tacitus	13
Gibson, Rev. Allan Sumner.—Aristotle's Organon	10
Goldie, J. H. D.—Boat Race Record	3
Hawkins (M.A.) E. L.—Aristotle's Ethics, Books I.-IV.	10
Hobbes, Thomas.—Leviathan	4
— Elements of Law	4
— Behemoth ; or, The Long Parliament	4
Iwan-Müller, E. B.—Literæ Humaniores	7
Justinian's Institutes, Analysis of	5
Jeyes (M.A.) S. H.—Classical Scholarships	6
— Cicero's Letters	12
— Juvenal	13
Joennies (Ph.D.) Ferdinand.—Hobbes's Behemoth	4
— Hobbes's Elements of Law	4
King, Rev. J. R.—Cicero's Philippics	12
— Cicero's Philippics, I. to IV.	12
— Cicero's Philippics, I. and II.	12
Lewis, Sir G. C.—Political Terms	4
— Government of Dependencies	4
Livy, Books V. to VII., Translation of	13
Marshall, Rev. Charles.—Latin Prayer Book	3
Marshall, W. W.—Plutarch's Lives of the Gracchi	13
— Latin Prayer Book	8
Ogle (M.A.) Rev. H. C.—Selected Pieces	8
— Latin Versions to Selected Pieces	8
Palæstra Oxoniensis	14 & 15
Peterson, Professor.—Cicero's Cluentius	12
Plato's Meno, Translation of	13
Poulton (M.A.) E. B.—Study Guide to Natural Science	7
Pulling (M.A.) F. S.—Oxford Study Guides	6
— Study Guide to History School	7
— Questions in English History	15
Questions, Algebraical	9
„ Arithmetical	9
„ in Advanced Logic	9
Simpson, F. P.—Demosthenes on the Crown	10
Skottowe, B. C.—Outlines of Constitutional History	5
Smith, Adam.—Wealth of Nations	5
Smith, Walter E.—Recent Depression of Trade	3
— Aristotle's Organon	10
Sparks, Rev. Fredrick.—School Arithmetic	7
Special Statutes, The	5
Thomas, J. L.—Trip to Italy and Attica	3
Treherne, G. G. T.—Boat Race Record	3
Walpole (M.A.) A. S.—Euripides Hecuba	13
Weatherley (M.A.) F. E.—Rudiments of Logic	9
— Questions on Logic	9
Williams, Rev. J. H.—Damon	5
Wilson (Bart., M.A.) Sir R. K.—Lewis's Political Terms	4
Wise, B. R.—Outlines of Jurisprudence	5
Woods (B.D.) Rev. F. H.—Canons of the Council of Orange	3
— Guide to the Theological School	6
Worcester J. B.—Livy's Second Punic War	13

www.ingramcontent.com/pod-product-compliance
Lightning Source LLC
Chambersburg PA
CBHW030333170426
43202CB00010B/1110